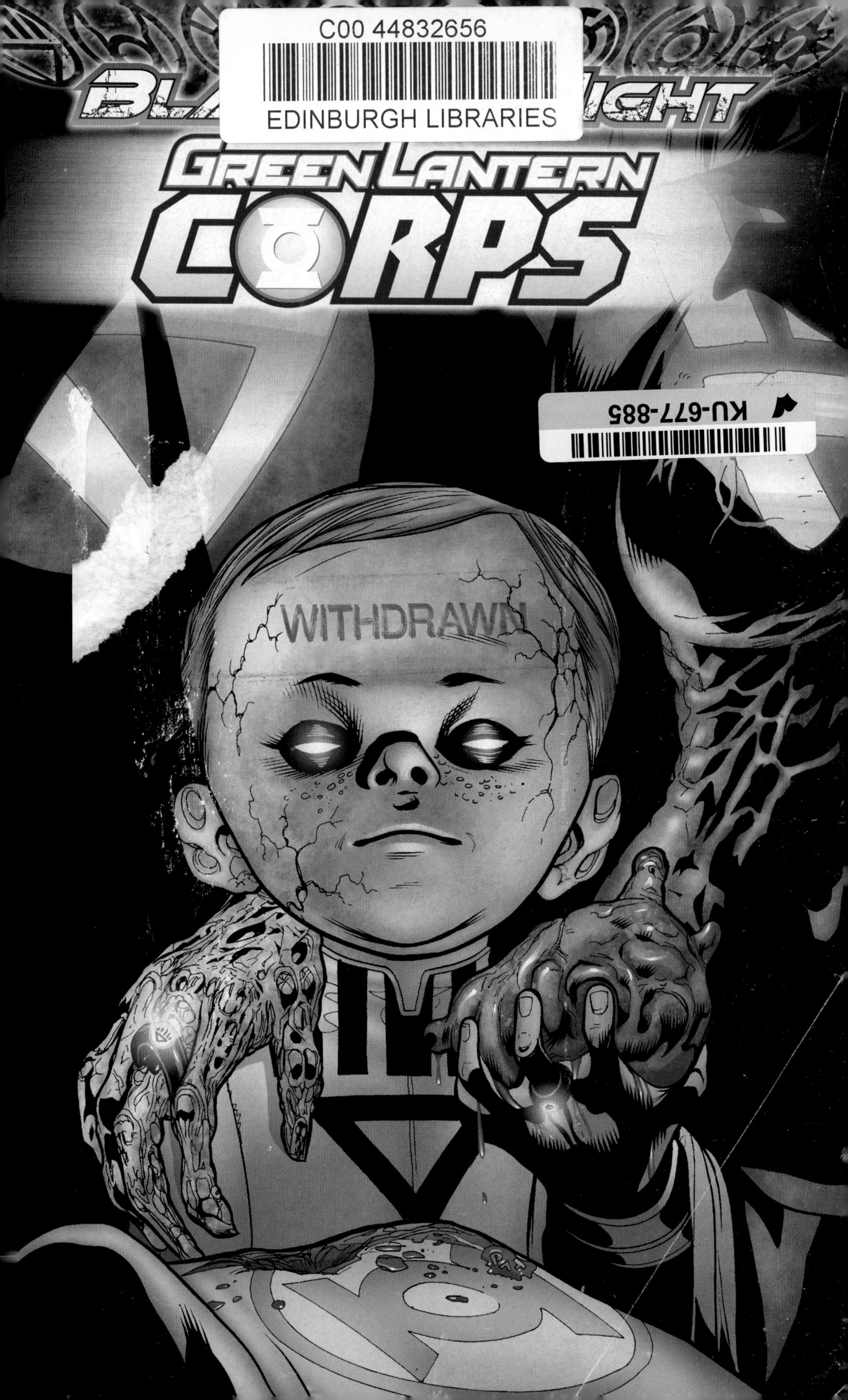
GREEN LANTERN
CORPS

Adam Schlagman *Editor-original series*
Bob Harras *Group Editor-Collected Editions* / Bob Joy *Editor*
Robbin Brosterman *Design Director-Books* / Curtis King Jr. *Senior Art Director*

DC COMICS / Diane Nelson *President* / Dan DiDio and Jim Lee *Co-Publishers*
Geoff Johns *Chief Creative Officer* / Patrick Caldon *EVP-Finance and Administration*
John Rood *EVP-Sales, Marketing and Business Development* / Amy Genkins *SVP-Business and Legal Affairs*
Steve Rotterdam *SVP-Sales and Marketing* / John Cunningham *VP-Marketing*
Terri Cunningham *VP-Managing Editor* / Alison Gill *VP-Manufacturing* / David Hyde *VP-Publicity*
Sue Pohja *VP-Book Trade Sales* / Alysse Soll *VP-Advertising and Custom Publishing*
Bob Wayne *VP-Sales* / Mark Chiarello *Art Director*

Cover by Rodolfo Migliari

BLACKEST NIGHT: GREEN LANTERN CORPS Published by DC Comics.

DC COMICS 1700 Broadway, New York, NY 10019 A Warner Bros. Entertainment Company

Printed by RR Donnelley, Salem, VA, USA. 6/10/11. First printing.

ISBN: 978-1-4012-2805-7

Fiber used in this product line meets the sourcing requirements of the SFI program.
www.sfiprogram.org SGS-SFI/COC-US10/81072

BLACKEST NIGHT

GREEN LANTERN CORPS

PETER J. TOMASI
WRITER

PATRICK GLEASON
PENCILS

REBECCA BUCHMAN
with TOM NGUYEN
PRENTIS ROLLINS
KEITH CHAMPAGNE
PATRICK GLEASON
MARK IRWIN
INKERS

RANDY MAYOR
GABE ELTAEB
COLORS

STEVE WANDS
LETTERS

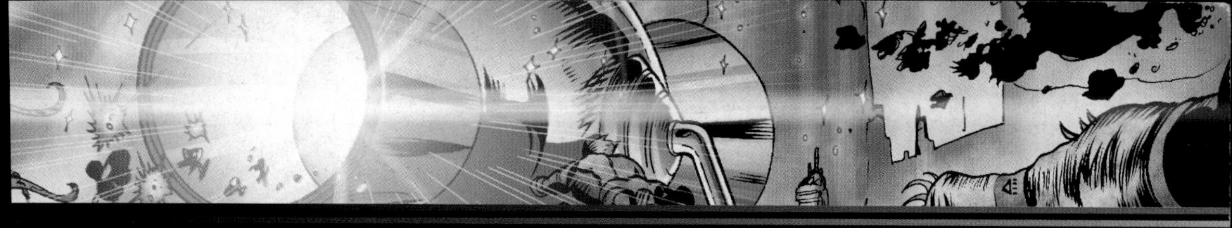

THE STORY SO FAR...

Billions of years ago, the self-appointed Guardians of the Universe recruited thousands of sentient beings from across the cosmos to join their intergalactic police force: the Green Lantern Corps.

Chosen because they are able to overcome great fear, the Green Lanterns patrol their respective space sectors armed with power rings capable of wielding the emerald energy of willpower into whatever constructs they can imagine.

Hal Jordan is the greatest of them all.

When the dying Green Lantern Abin Sur crashed on Earth, he chose Hal Jordan to be his successor, for his indomitable will and ability to overcome great fear. As the protector of Sector 2814, Hal has saved Earth from destruction, even died in its service and been reborn.

Thaal Sinestro of Korugar was once considered the greatest Green Lantern of them all.

As Abin Sur's friend, Sinestro became Jordan's mentor in the Corps. But after being sentenced to the Anti-Matter Universe for abusing his power, Sinestro learned of the yellow light of fear being mined on Qward. Wielding a new golden power ring fueled by terror, Sinestro drafted thousands of the most horrific, psychotic and sadistic beings in the universe, and with their doctrine of fear, burned all who opposed them.

When the Green Lantern Corps battled their former ally during the Sinestro Corps War, the skies burned with green and gold as Earth erupted into an epic battle between good and evil. Though the Green Lanterns won, their brotherhood was broken and the peace they achieved was short-lived. In its aftermath, the Guardians rewrote the Book of Oa, the very laws by which their corps abides, and dissent grew within their members.

Now Hal Jordan will face his greatest challenge yet, as the prophecy foretold by Abin Sur in his dying moments finally comes to pass...

The emotional spectrum has splintered into seven factions. Seven corps were born.

The Green Lanterns. The Sinestro Corps. Atrocitus and the enraged Red Lanterns. Larfleeze, the avaricious keeper of the Orange Light. Former Guardians Ganthet and Sayd's small but hopeful Blue Lantern Corps. The Zamarons and their army of fierce and loving Star Sapphires. And the mysterious Indigo Tribe.

As the War of Light ignited between these Lantern bearers, the skies on every world darkened. In Sector 666, on the planet Ryut, a black lantern grew around the Anti-Monitor's corpse, using his vast energies to empower it.

The first of the Black Lanterns, the Black Hand, has risen from the dead, heralding a greater power that will extinguish all of the light—and life—in the universe.

Now across thousands of worlds, the dead have risen, and Hal Jordan and all of Earth's greatest heroes must bear witness to Blackest Night, which will descend upon them all, without prejudice, mercy or reason.

GREEN LANTERN CORPS 39
Cover by Patrick Gleason and Christian Alamy with Randy Mayor

FADE TO BLACK

PATRICK GLEASON

PENCILS

REBECCA BUCHMAN
TOM NGUYEN

INKS

SECTOR 0.
GUESS IT WORKED OUT IN THE END BEING BEAM-SLAPPED BY THE GUARDIANS BACK TO EARTH. AT LEAST WE GOT TO BE THERE FOR TRIBUTE DAY.
AND AT LEAST WE GOT TO BE THERE FOR HAL IN COAST CITY.
YOU DID GET TO SEE ICE, RIGHT?
YEAH, AT BLUE BEETLE'S GRAVE IN CHICAGO. TOOK HER TO DINNER-- TALKED A LOT--
SOMEPLACE NICE, I HOPE?
"ABSOLUTELY.
"WHAT KINDA KNUCKLEDRAGGER DO YA TAKE ME FOR?"
AIN'T WRIGGLEY FIELD GREAT AT NIGHT, CHECK OUT ALL THE IVY.
AND?
AND I MISS HER-- A LOT. THIS BEING A COUPLE MILLION MILES AWAY THING...
STILL NOT WORKING TOO GOOD, HUH, GUY?
AS A MATTER OF FACT, KYLE, IT SUCKS.
AND I'M GUESSING I KNOW WHERE YOU WENT FOR TRIBUTE DAY.
AND WHERE'S THAT?
VALHALLA.
AREN'T YOU A REGULAR DETECTIVE CHIMP.
"I SAW JADE'S STATUE AT THE CEMETERY--SAW HER FATHER--PAID MY RESPECTS, AND NOW HERE I AM."
JADE
AND EVERYBODY KNOWS THAT HERE IS NOWHERE.
WHAT'S THAT SUPPOSED TO MEAN?
MEANS THAT IF YOUR HEART'S NOT HERE, YOU'RE NOT HERE.

"REMEMBER A WHILE BACK I WAS TELLING YOU ABOUT HOW THAT STAR SAPPHIRE SHOWED ME WHO MY SUPPOSED TRUE LOVE WAS?"
"YEAH."
"WELL, THE SAPPHIRE SHOWED ME IT WAS JADE, AND I LIED TO SOMEONE I CARE ABOUT AND TOLD HER THAT IT WAS--"
"AND THIS SOMEONE YOU CARE ABOUT IS SORANIK?"
IT'S THAT OBVIOUS, HUH?
ONLY TO SOMEONE WHO KNOWS YA.
I KNOW IT'S AGAINST ONE OF THE LAWS BUT--
SCREW THE LAWS, THE GUARDIANS ARE MAKING 'EM UP NOW AS THEY GO ALONG.
I'M STILL WEARING THIS RING FOR THE SAME REASON YOU ARE, AND *THAT'S* TO DO GOOD AND SAVE PEOPLE'S ASSES.
I'M SURE AS HELL NOT DOING IT TO BE IN THE GOOD GRACES OF THOSE BLUEBIRDS.
NOW LISTEN, I DON'T WANT THIS TO SOUND COLD, BUDDY, BUT JADE'S DEAD AND SORANIK'S ALIVE, AND IT LOOKS TO ME LIKE YOU'RE AMONG THE LIVING FOR NOW SO CASE CLOSED.
BUT MAYBE SEEING JADE IN THAT SAPPHIRE IS A WAY OF ASKING MYSELF WHETHER I--
BUT NOTHIN'--THE HEAR THAT'S *BEATING* IS TH ONE YOU JUMP OFF TH CLIFF FOR.
YOU SEE THAT?
YEP, TWO GREENIES COMING UP AT 12 O' CLOCK.

HEY, LADIES, MIND IF WE JOIN YA?
OF COURSE NOT, LANTERN GARDNER.
GREETINGS, LANTERN RAYNER.

LANTERN NATU. LANTERN IOLANDE. IT'S GOOD TO SEE YOU'RE BOTH WELL.
LANTERN RAYNER. LANTERN GARDNER.
HOW'S KORUGAR HANDLING THE SINESTRO SITUATION?

EMOTIONS WERE HIGH AFTER THE EXECUTION WAS CANCELLED BUT OTHERWISE--
LANTERN NATU NOT ONLY DIALED BACK THE CIVIL UNREST, SHE ALSO MANAGED TO--
JUGGLE SEVERAL SURGERIES WHILE I WAS THERE TOO.
UM, YES, A MASTER JUGGLER, OUR LANTERN NATU.

HEADING IN FOR MOP-UP OPS, HUH?
"MOP-UP OPS"?
YEAH, THE CLEANUP ON OA.

WHAT HAS TO BE CLEANED UP?
HAVEN'T YOU RECEIVED ANY UPDATES ABOUT THE SCIENCELL BREAKOUT?

NO, OUR RINGS HAVE BEEN QUIET-- WE'VE ACTUALLY HAD NO REPORTS FROM OA ABOUT ANY KIND OF UNUSUAL--

--ACTIVITY.
THE OAN BATTERY SHELL-- IT'S--
WARNING. IMMINENT DANGER. RAPIDLY APPROACHING OBJECTS DETECTED. SHIELDS TO FULL POWER.

IT'S A LONG STORY WHICH WE OBVIOUSLY DON'T HAVE TIME FOR.

OBJECTS-- WHAT KIND OF OBJECTS?
UNKNOWN POWER RINGS.
POWER RINGS?

AH, FER THE LOVE A'--

FLSSH
FLSSH
FLSSH
FLSSH
FLSSH
FLSSH
FLSSH
FLSSH

FZSSH
FZSSH
FZSSH
FZSSH
FZSSH
FZSSH
FZSSH

FLSSH

FLSSH

FLSSH

AN UNKNOWN PLANET IN SECTOR 3599.
MAMA! PLEASE! WHERE ARE YOU?!?
HOW COULD YOU LEAVE US ALONE?
WE'RE HUNGRY, MOTHER.
...SO HUNGRY...
...IT HURTS, MAMA...
...HUNGRY...
ZAMARON.
MAINTAIN. YOUR. COMPOSURE. KRYB.
I. WILL. HAVE. YOU. FREE. FROM. THIS. ZAMARON. CRYSTAL. SOON.
ARRRR!
WHY WON'T YOU FEED US, MAMA?
WHY WON'T YOU BRING US FOOD LIKE YOU USED TO?
ARE YOU MAD AT US, MAMA?
PLEASE DON'T BE MAD.
WE'RE SORRY IF WE MADE YOU MAD.
MAMA DON'T GOOOOOOO!
MAMA COME HOME!

KORUGAR. SECTOR 1415.
FIRST IMPRESSIONS, AS THEY SAY, ARE EVERYTHING, KORUGAR.
I WANTED TO MAKE ONE ON YOU IMMEDIATELY.
IT'S THE ONE AND ONLY PROPER CHOICE TO MAKE IF YOU, AS A RACE, WANT TO CONTINUE PROPAGATING.
IN FACT, I APPLAUD YOU.
IN MY...TRAVELS, THERE HAVE BEEN MANY WHO HAVE CHOSEN EXTINCTION OVER EXISTENCE.
BUT, TO EACH HIS OWN.
AS YOU CAN SEE I'M NOT EXACTLY AVERSE TO DISPENSING...LIFE LESSONS WHEN DEEMED NECESSARY.
A LESSON TO DISSUADE YOU FROM RAISING A HAND IN VIOLENCE AGAINST THE SINESTRO CORPS AND ME.

AND AS YOU CAN SEE, YOUR MAIN AVENUE IS AS LONG AS IT IS WIDE...
...PLENTY OF SPACE TO CONTINUE "POSTING" YOUR FELLOW KORUGARIANS AS LESSONS TO YOU ALL HERE AT THE NEW BASE OF...
...THE MONGUL CORPS!

SOMETHING YOU CAN SMELL...
YOU CAN SEE WITH YOUR OWN EYES THAT--RIGHT FROM THE START--ALLOWS YOU TO RECOGNIZE THE NATURAL ORDER OF THINGS FROM HERE ON OUT.
SUBMISSION AND PROSTRATION BEFORE YOUR BETTERS IS NOT A CRIME.
COME TO THINK OF IT--I DO BELIEVE IT'S TIME FOR A NAME CHANGE OF THIS ORGANIZA--
KRAK
LEAVE US BE, YOU DESTROYER OF WORLDS!
ONCE LANTERN SORANIK NATU, THE SAVIOR OF KORUGAR, HEARS OF YOUR HORRIBLE DEEDS, SHE AND THE GREEN LANTERN CORPS WILL--
"LANTERN NATU"?
SORRY, THE NAME ESCAPES ME.
AS FOR THE GREEN LANTERN CORPS--LET THEM COME AND LET THEM DIE.
I DO THINK IT'S TIME YOU EMBRACE THIS NEW SITUATION YOU'RE IN FROM A NEW PERSPECTIVE.
I AM THE SAVIOR OF KORUGAR.
AAIEEE!
ZZRAKK

OA.
LET'S TRY TO CUT THESE THINGS OFF AT THE PASS!
GO TO AFTERBURNERS!

ALL RIGHT, LET'S SEE 'EM GET--
FLSSH
FLSSH
FLSSH
--THROUGH THAT.
AW, CRAP.
AW, CRAP.
OT SURE WHAT VE GOT HERE, UT IT CAN'T BE GOOD!
LET'S GET DOWN THERE!
IOLANDE AND I ARE GOING STRAIGHT TO THE HOSPITAL TO GET THE PATIENTS TO SAFETY!
BE CAREFUL, KYLE.
YOU TOO.
THAT'S IT, "YOU TOO"? WHY DIDN'T YOU TELLA THAT NICE GIRLA: I LOVEYA SO MUCHA, NATU, I THINK I'MA GONNA DIE!
ZIP IT.

CAN'T RAISE ANYBODY-- SOME KINDA RING INTERFERENCE-- ALMOST LIKE WE'RE BEING JAMMED.
WE NEED A RALLYING POINT FAST! LET'S GET TO THE CENTRAL POWER BATTERY!
HEADS UP, LANTERNS!
WE JUST GOT HIT BY A STORM OF BLACK RINGS JUST OUTSIDE OF OA'S ORBIT--!
BLACK RINGS?
YEAH, KILOWOG, THEY WENT THROUGH A SHIELD CONSTRUCT WE THREW UP LIKE IT WAS TISSUE PAPER.
WITH THE OAN BATTERY SHELL GONE, THERE'S NOTHING TO STOP--
--GUY, YOU HEAR THAT?
WHAT?
SOUNDS LIKE FLIES.

STAND YOUR GROUND, POOZERS!
RAISE SHIELDS--WE DON'T KNOW WHAT WE'RE DEALING WITH HERE!
FLSSH
FLSSH
DAMMIT! THEY'RE IN!
EVERYONE--KEEP SHIELDS AT FULL STRENGTH!
FLSSH
FLSSH
FLSSH
FLSSH
FLSSH
FLSSH
WHAT THE HELL--THE BLACK RINGS AREN'T ATTACKING US--THEY'RE ZEROING IN...
...ON THE LANTERN CRYPT!
SALAAK! GET THE BLUE GUYS ON THE HORN!
I AM TRYING, BUT THEY ARE NOT RESPONDING.
WE'LL HEAD TO THE CRYPT TO HELP MORRO--YOU HEAD TO THE CITADEL AND FIND OUT WHY THE GUARDIANS AREN'T PICKING UP THE PHONE!

THE CRYPT OF THE GREEN LANTERN CORPS.
SKRAW
SKRAW
UNKNOWN POWER RINGS PENETRATING LEVEL FOUR.
UNKNOWN POWER RINGS PENETRATING LEVEL THREE.
UNKNOWN POWER RINGS PENETRATING LEVEL TWO.
I KNOW, MY FRIENDS.
BUT WE WILL DO WHAT WE MUST.
UNKNOWN POWER RINGS PENETRATING LEVEL ONE.
YES, THE UPDATE IS MUCH APPRECIATED.
FOUL ABERRATIONS!
FLESH.
FLESH.
FLESH.
FLESH.
FLESH.
FLESH.
FLESH.
FLESH.
YOU DARE BREACH THE SANCTITY OF THE CRYPT?!

KATMA TUI OF KORUGAR.
SKRAK
SACRILEGE!
THESE HONORED DEAD DESERVE THEIR PEACE!
AND I...
...MORRO THE CRYPTKEEPER...
SKRAW
JACK T. CHANCE OF GARNET.
...WILL MAKE SURE THEY GET IT!

FWOOM
NO...
TOMAR-RE OF XANDOR.
NOOOOO!
LEAVE THEM BE!
RISE

HOLY CRAP, E WALLS OF THE RYPT LOOK LIKE CHUNK OF SWISS CHEESE!
WE BETTER GET DOWN THERE BEFORE--
SKRAW
SKRAW
SKRAW
MORRO'S ALIVE! HIS DRATURES GOT HIM OUT OF THERE.
WHAT THE #@$%?
RING, WHAT ARE WE LOOKING AT?
RAGE.
WILL.
WILL.
ALL DECEASED GREEN LANTERNS WITHIN CRYPT HAVE BEEN COMPROMISED.

ALL DECEASED GREEN LANTERNS NOW RESURRECTED.
ALL ARE NOW BLACK LANTERNS.
HELLO, KYLE, MY LOVE.
GOD... NO...

OKAY, I'M REALLY NOT SURE HOW THIS CAN GET ANY FREAKIN' WORSE!

JADE!
IT'S TIME FOR YOU TO REALIZE, KYLE, THAT...
...TWO HEARTS ARE BETTER THAN ONE.

GREEN LANTERN CORPS 40
Cover by Patrick Gleason and Rebecca Buchman with Randy Mayor

HEART OF DARKNESS

PATRICK GLEASON
PENCILS

REBECCA BUCHMAN
TOM NGUYEN
PRENTIS ROLLINS
INKS

SECTOR 0.
ARISIA RRAB. GREEN LANTERN OF SECTOR 2815.
AFTER EVERYTHING THAT'S HAPPENED ON DAXAM...
...ALL THE DEATH...
...ALL THE HORROR...
...IT REALLY HITS ME...
...MY...PARTNER'S DEAD.

SODAM FLEW INTO THE SUN TO SAVE HIS PLANET.
AND I LEFT HIM THERE.
ALONE.
BURNING.
FOREVER.

RING.
WHERE'S THE OAN SHELL, WHAT DID I MISS?
INFORMATION LIMITED. IT NO LONGER EXISTS.
BEEN TRYING TO UPLOAD MY ACTION REPORT TO LANTERN SALAAK AND TELL EVERYONE THE SAD NEWS, BUT I CAN'T GET THROUGH.
COMMUNICATIONS DIAGNOSIS IN PROGRESS.

WELL, NO MATTER WHAT, ALL I KNOW IS THAT I'M GLAD TO BE BACK WHERE I DON'T HAVE TO WIPE THE BLOOD FROM MY GLOVES AND SMELL THE STENCH OF BURNING BODIES WITH EVERY BREATH I TAKE.
AT LEAST ON OA THERE'S A LITTLE PEACE AND QUIET AND EVERYONE'S...

...NOT TRYING TO KILL EACH OTHER.

THERE'S DADDY'S LITTLE GIRL!
DA?
WE'VE BEEN LOOKING ALL OVER FOR YOU.
WE'RE SO GLAD WE FINALLY FOUND YOU, ARISIA.
MA?
IT'S BEEN TOO LONG SINCE WE'VE BEEN ALL TOGETHER AS A FAMILY.
I DON'T UNDERSTAND...
...YOU LOOK DIFFERENT...BUT THE SAME...
IS IT REALLY YOU?
LOVE.
HOPE.
FEAR.
OF COURSE IT'S REALLY US, ARISIA. WHO ELSE WOULD YOU EXPECT US TO BE?
THAT'S RIGHT, DARLING.
GRANDPA SANTARA?
I DO
I AGREE!
THE FAMILY THAT FEEDS TOGETHER STAYS TOGETHER.
NO--WAIT--STAY BACK--PLEASE GET AWAY--

JADE...
JENNIE...
...IT CAN'T BE...
BLOCK OUT EVERYTHING AROUND US FOR THE MOMENT.
LOOK AT ME, MY LOVE.
ARE THESE MY EYES YOU'RE STARING INTO, KYLE?
YES.
ARE THESE THE LIPS YOU'VE KISSED?
YES.
LOVE.
WILL.
IS THIS MY VOICE, KYLE?
YES... BUT...
BUT NOTHING.
LET'S GO HIGHER...
...ABOVE THE DISTRACTIONS.
WHERE WE CAN L OUR LOV RISE ABOV ALL THIS DARKNES

KYLE, I UNDERSTAND HOW STRANGE THIS ALL SEEMS...
...BUT I'M HERE *BECAUSE* OF YOU.
YOU BROUGHT ME HERE.

HOW DID I BRING YOU HERE?
YOUR UNDYING LOVE FOR ME.
IT'S ANCHORED ME.
KEPT ME WARM.

WANTING...
...NEEDING...
...YOUR TOUCH HAS KEPT ME WARMER.

JEN...
EVERYTHING WE SHARED TOGETHER.
OUR LIVES.
OUR HEARTS.
OUR SOULS.
LOVE NEVER DIES.

LOVE.
COMPASSION.
WILL.
AND THE HEART NEVER LIES.

SECTOR 3599.
YOUR MOTHER'S COMING, MY LITTLE ONES.
I WILL FEED YOU--HOLD YOU--LOVE YOU WITH EVERY FIBER OF MY BEING.
BUT PLEASE--TALK TO ME--WHY CAN'T I HEAR YOU ANYMORE, MY DARLINGS?
YOUR SWEET VOICES...HAVE FALLEN QUIET...
...THE SILENCE IS DEAFENING...
...IT'S TOO MUCH TO BE--ARRGGGH!
YOU THINK YOU COULD ESCAPE SO EASILY FROM THE CRYSTALS?!?
I'VE CHASED YOU ACROSS FOUR STAR-FIELDS.
YOU'RE GOING BACK TO ZAMARON WHERE QUEEN AGA'PO WILL SEE TO IT THAT--
PLEASE... I BEG YOU...
...MY CHILDREN ARE DYING OF HUNGER BACK ON MY PLANET--THEY NEED ME--
SEARCH MY HEART, YOU'LL SEE I'M TELLING YOU THE TRUTH--LET ME SAVE THEM--I'LL WILLINGLY COME BACK TO ZAMARON IF YOU LET ME GO TO THEM NOW--PLEASE...
YOUR LOVE AND CONCERN FOR THE CHILDREN BURNS BRIGHT. YOU SPEAK ONLY THE TRUTH.
THOUGH WHAT YOU'VE DONE UP TO THIS POINT WITH YOUR LIFE DISGUSTS ME, SAVING THESE CHILDREN IS NOW OUR PRIORITY.
I WILL ESCORT YOU BACK TO TEND TO THEM, THEN OUR TRUCE WILL BE OVER.
THANK YOU, SAPPHIRE.
YOUR KINDNESS WON'T BE FORGOTTEN.

OA
PLANETARY CITADEL OF THE GUARDIANS OF THE UNIVERSE.
OKAY, LANTERN SALAAK, TELL US THESE EIGHT BLACK SPLOTCHES OF GOOP ISN'T ALL THAT'S LEFT OF THE GUARDIANS OF THE UNIVERSE.
RING, IS THIS AN ORGANIC SUBSTANCE BELONGING TO THE GUARDIANS?
NEGATIVE. THE RESIDUAL SUBSTANCE DOES NOT BELONG TO THE GUARDIANS.
WHAT IS IT THEN?
UNKNOWN.
LOOK AT THE OUTLINE OF THE BODIES.
IT'S LIKE THEY WERE SLAMMED INTO THE WALL ALL IN THE SAME WAY--THEIR ARMS AND LEGS SPREAD WIDE--
AS IF THEY WERE BEING FORCED AGAINST THEIR WILL--LIKE PRISONERS.
WE ARE SPEAKING ABOUT THE GUARDIANS OF THE UNIVERSE, LANTERN ISAMOT.
WHAT COULD POSSIBLY BIND THEM AGAINST THEIR RESOLVE, THEIR COMBINED POWER--
WASN'T ABLE TO HELP EVEN THEM.
AND WE'VE GOT ANOTHER PROBLEM.
DID ANYONE COUNT THE NUMBER OF BLACK MARKS ON THE WALL?
THERE'S EIGHT HERE. LAST TIME I CHECKED THERE WERE NINE GUARDIANS.

THE FIRST THING WE NEED TO--
STEP AWAY, SALAAK.
ALL SCANS COMPLETE.
THE GUARDIANS ARE NOWHERE ON OA.
FROM THIS MOMENT FORTH, THE GUARDIANS' PLANETARY CITADEL IS A CRIME SCENE.
AND WE, THE ALPHA LANTERNS, ARE NOW IN CHARGE OF OA.
"IN CHARGE"?!?
YOU ARE IN CHARGE OF NOTHING!

WE ARE THE ALPHA LANTERNS, AND WE ARE THE LAW HERE ON OA ONCE A VACUUM OF LEADERSHIP PRESENTS ITSELF DUE TO UNFORESEEN OR CATASTROPHIC CIRCUMSTANCES.
AND THESE RECENT EVENTS CAN MOST DEFINITELY BE DEFINED AS CATASTROPHIC.
WE ARE THE ONES WHO HAVE BEEN CHARGED BY THE GUARDIANS THEMSELVES WITH MAINTAINING ORDER NOT ONLY WITHIN THE RANKS OF THE CORPS ITSELF BUT THROUGHOUT OA, SO AS OF THIS MOMENT --
YOU'VE BEEN GIVEN NO SUCH POWER, AND YOU ARE QUITE DELUSIONAL ABOUT THE BREADTH OF YOUR AUTHORITY.
ALLOW ME TO ENLIGHTEN YOU.
IF THIS HOLOGRAM HAS BEEN ACTIVATED, IT IS BECAUSE THE CORPS FINDS ITSELF IN A DIRE SITUATION AND WE, THE GUARDIANS OF THE UNIVERSE, ARE UNABLE TO PERFORM OUR SACRED DUTY AT THIS TIME.
THE SUCCESSION OF COMMAND IS AS FOLLOWS: CLARISSI AND THEN THE ILLUSTRES.
IT IS NOT SIMPLY OUR DIRECTIVE, BUT THE LAW OF OA. SEE THAT IT IS FOLLOWED.
AND JUST IN CASE YOU DON'T REMEMBER, I AM THE CLARISSI AND LANTERNS GARDNER AND RAYNER ARE THE CURRENT ILLUSTRES HONOR GUARDS.

THERE'S AN OLD MILITARY ADAGE THAT WE LEARNED BACK IN THE RANNIAN ARMY. SOME EARTHLING ONCE SAID IT:
IF YOU WANT A WAR, THEN LET IT BEGIN RIGHT HERE.
I'D LISTEN TO HIM, BECAUSE IF THERE IS ONE THING VATH SARN LIKES MORE THAN ANYTHING, IT'S WAR.
VEILED THREATS WILL NOT BE TOLERATED AT--
THIS IS NO VEILED THREAT. THIS IS THE LAW.
YOU FOLLOWED THE GUARDIANS' DECREE WHEN YOU EXECUTED THE SCIENCELLS PRISONERS AND YOU WILL FOLLOW IT NOW.
YOU DO NOT PICK AND CHOOSE TO FOLLOW A LAW WHEN IT SUITS YOU AND YOUR NEEDS.
THESE STANDOFFS BETWEEN GREEN LANTERNS AND ALPHA LANTERNS SEEM TO BE COMMON OCCURRENCES OF LATE.
IT ENDS RIGHT HERE AND NOW.
I'M NOT USUALLY FOND OF QUOTING HIM, BUT AS LANTERN GARDNER WOULD SAY IN HIS OWN INIMITABLE WAY:
GET YOUR RED AND BLUE METAL ASSES OUT OF HERE AND DEFEND OA AND THE CORPS AGAINST THOSE VILE ABOMINATIONS BEFORE THERE IS NOTHING LEFT!
THIS IS ONE CORPS AND WE WILL ACT AS ONE CORPS!
MY FIRST COMMAND DECISION IS THAT A MORATORIUM NOW EXISTS ON THE REISSUING OF POWER RINGS OF DECEASED LANTERNS AND THE FORGING OF NEW RINGS.
RECRUITS WILL NOT BE PUT IN MORTAL JEOPARDY. ALL EXISTING RINGS WITHOUT BEARERS WILL BE SENT TO MOGO UNTIL THE TENUOUS SITUATION HERE HAS BEEN STABILIZED TO MY SATISFACTION.

KYLE.
WE CAN HAVE WHAT WE ONCE HAD.
AND THIS TIME IT NEVER HAS TO END.
YOU'VE SEEN THE FACE OF TRUE LOVE...
...AND IT WAS MINE, WASN'T IT?
YOU LOVED ME THEN AND YOU LOVE ME NOW.
MY HEART MAY WANT TO BELIEVE THAT THIS IS YOU--BUT MY HEAD KNOWS BETTER.
WHATEVER YOU ARE-- YOU'RE NOT MY JENNIE LYNN.
SHE'S GONE.
I WATCHED HER DIE TRYING TO SAVE THE UNIVERSE.

YOU'RE *ONE* OF THOSE *THINGS* THAT'S DOWN THERE ON OA HURTING MY FRIENDS AND DESTROYING EVERYTHING I CARE ABOUT...
...AND THE ONLY REASON I LET YOU BABBLE ON AND HAVE A GO AT TRYING TO SEDUCE ME WAS TO FIGURE OUT EXACTLY WHAT THE HELL YOU AND THESE BLACK LANTERNS ARE AFTER.

BUT YOU KNOW WHAT, RIGHT NOW I DON'T GIVE A DAMN ABOUT ANYTHING...

...EXCEPT CAUSING YOU SOME MASSIVE PAIN!
FRAZZAKK

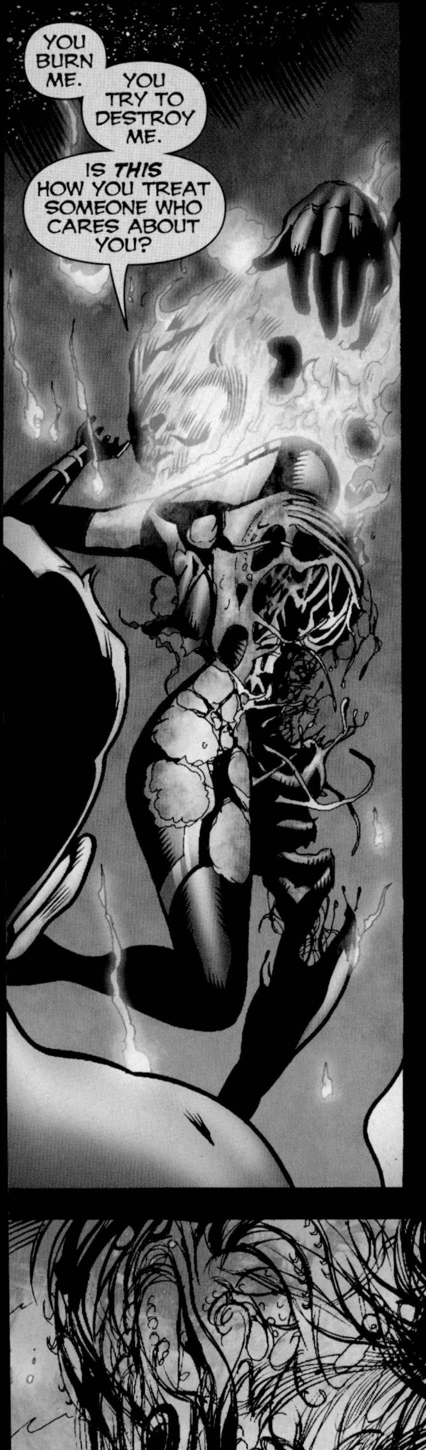
YOU BURN ME.
YOU TRY TO DESTROY ME.
IS *THIS* HOW YOU TREAT SOMEONE WHO CARES ABOUT YOU?

NO, THIS IS HOW I TREAT SOMEONE WHO DARES TO DISHONOR AND DISGRACE THE MEMORY AND REMAINS OF A WOMAN I CARED DEEPLY FOR!
FRAZZAAKK

WELL, KYLE...

...IF I CAN'T GET YOU TO LOVE ME...

...MAYBE I CAN GET YOU TO FEAR ME!
UNNF!
FOR SOMEONE WHO'S SAVED A LOT OF STRANGERS OVER THE YEARS...
...YOU HAVEN'T DONE TOO WELL PROTECTING THE PEOPLE YOU ACTUALLY CARED ABOUT, HMM?
YAARGH!

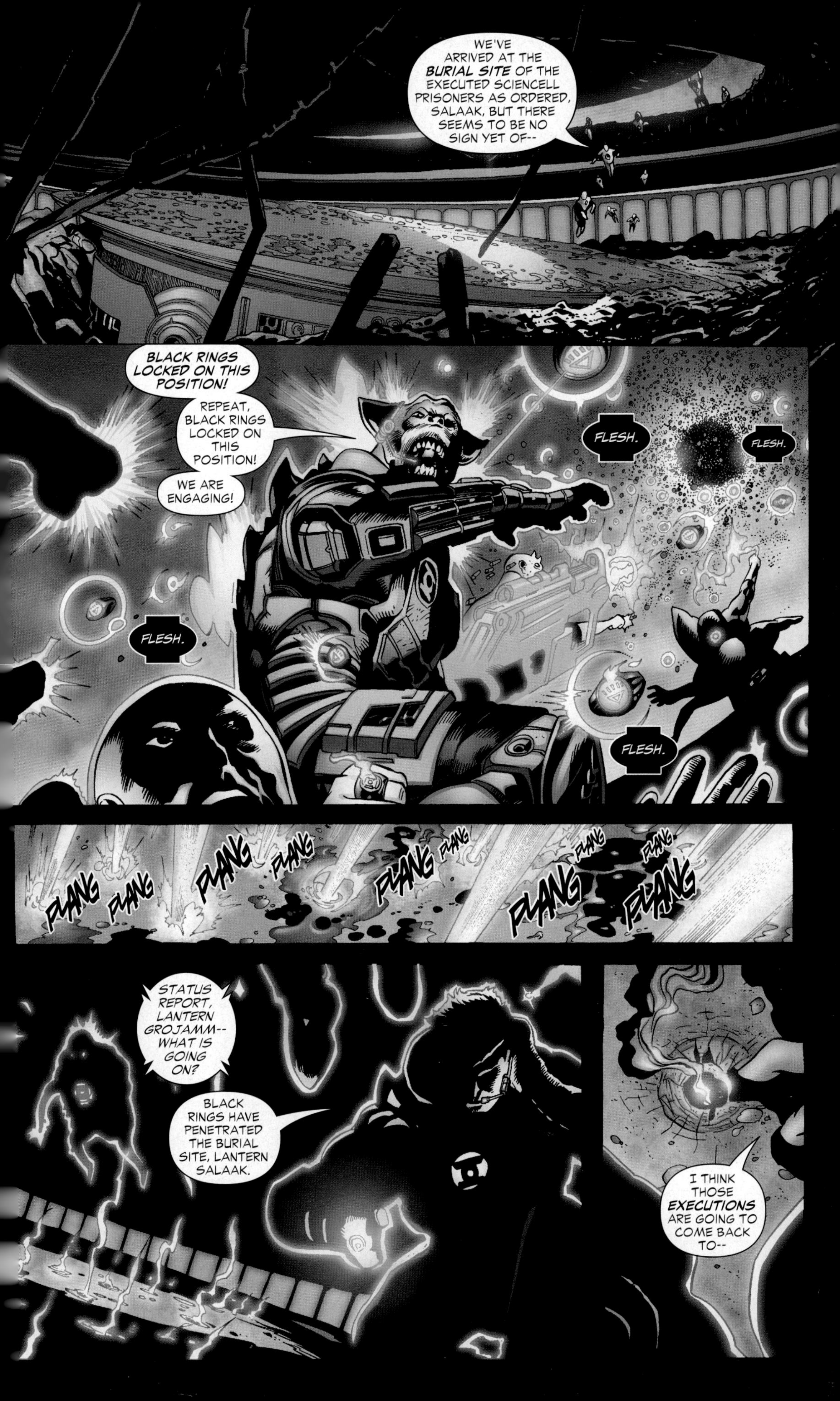
WE'VE ARRIVED AT THE BURIAL SITE OF THE EXECUTED SCIENCELL PRISONERS AS ORDERED, SALAAK, BUT THERE SEEMS TO BE NO SIGN YET OF--
BLACK RINGS LOCKED ON THIS POSITION!
REPEAT, BLACK RINGS LOCKED ON THIS POSITION!
WE ARE ENGAGING!
FLESH.
FLESH.
FLESH.
FLESH.
PLANG PLANG PLANG PLANG PLANG PLANG PLANG PLANG PLANG PLANG PLANG
STATUS REPORT, LANTERN GROJAMM-- WHAT IS GOING ON?
BLACK RINGS HAVE PENETRATED THE BURIAL SITE, LANTERN SALAAK.
I THINK THOSE EXECUTIONS ARE GOING TO COME BACK TO--

--HAUNT US!
RAGE.
FEAR.
WILL.
RAGE.
WILL.
FEAR.
RAGE.
POWER LEVELS 45.96%
NO RING BEARER CHOSEN. PROCEED TO MOGO IN SECTOR 2261.
NO RING BEARER CHOSEN. PROCEED TO MOGO IN SECTOR 2261.
NO RING BEARER CHOSEN. PROCEED TO MOG IN SECTOR 2261.
POWER LEVELS 45.97%

TIME TO DIE, LANTERN.
I'LL FIGHT YOU WITH MY LAST--
...LANTERN TUI...IS THAT YOU...?
...THANK YOU FOR SAVING--
--BREATH--
--MEEEee
NO RING BEARER CHOSEN. PROCEED TO MOGO IN SECTOR 2261.
POWER LEVELS 46.09%

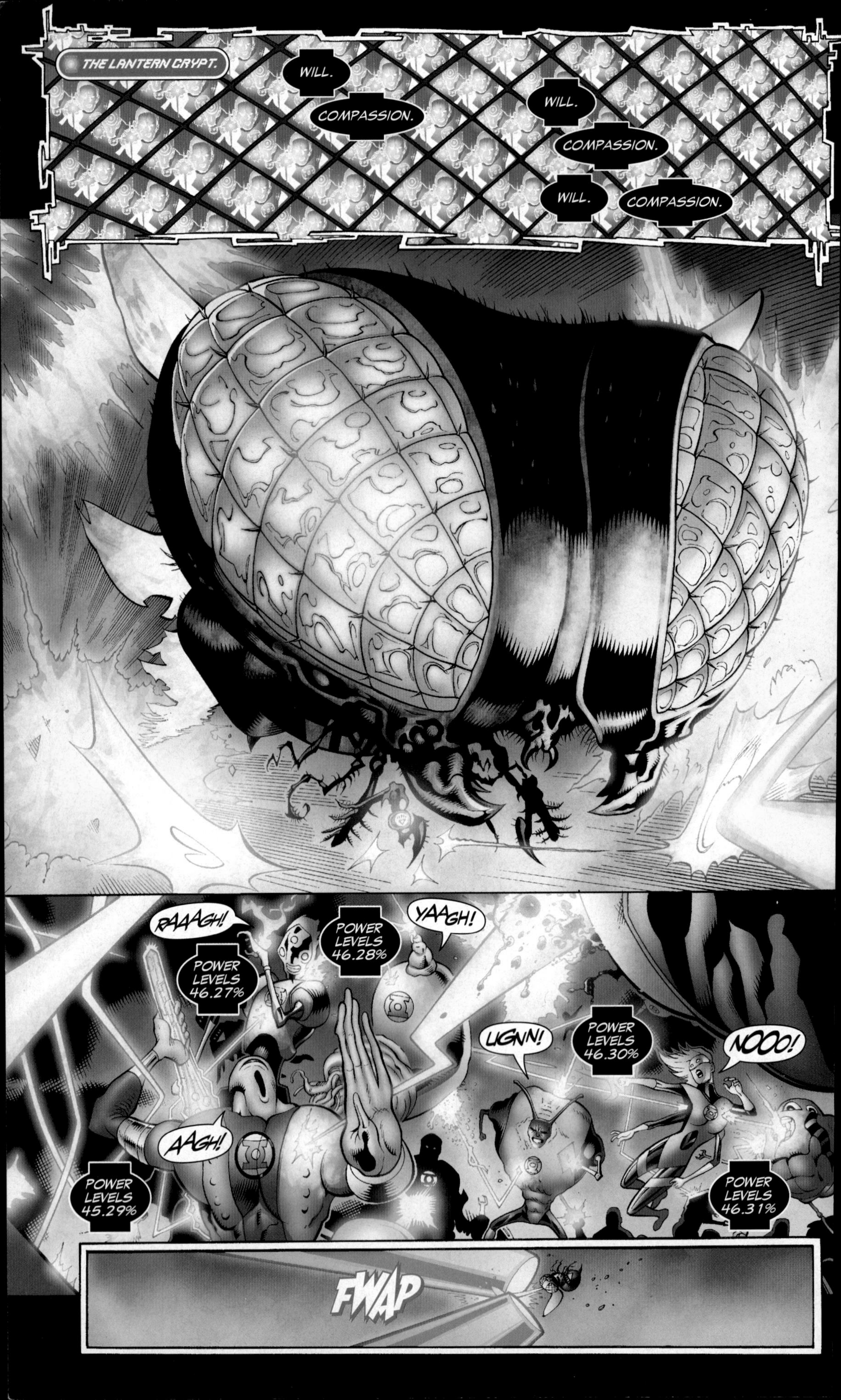
THE LANTERN CRYPT.
WILL.
COMPASSION.
WILL.
COMPASSION.
WILL.
COMPASSION.
RAAAGH!
POWER LEVELS 46.27%
POWER LEVELS 46.28%
YAAGH!
UGNN!
POWER LEVELS 46.30%
NOOO!
AAGH!
POWER LEVELS 45.29%
POWER LEVELS 46.31%
FWAP

WHAT THE HELL ARE YOU DOING, BZZD, YOU'RE KILLING FELLOW LANTERNS IN COLD BLOOD?!?
YOU SAVED US FROM MONGUL BACK ON THE MERCY PLANET!
YOU GAVE YOUR LIFE FOR OURS, BZZD!
THIS ISN'T YOU, DAMN IT! FIGHT! DON'T LET WHATEVER'S DOING THIS TAKE CONTROL!
I WAS JUST THE DIMINUTIVE LANTERN, I COULD NEVER MEASURE UP TO THE MIGHTY HONOR GUARD GUY GARDNER.
THE JOKES AND BELITTLING AT MY EXPENSE...
SEEMS ONLY IN DEATH AM I FINALLY WORTHY OF YOUR RESPECT.
BUT THE IRONY NOW IS I NO LONGER WANT OR CARE ABOUT YOUR RESPECT, GARDNER...
...NOW I ONLY WANT YOUR HEART!

RRRNNN!
AARGGH!
ZZZRRRASH
ARGGG!
SORRY, BZZD!
SKRAZZAAAKK

IT WAS EITHER YOU OR--
NEXT TIME PICK ON SOMEONE...
SHUNK
...YOUR OWN SIZE, GARDNER!
AARGHHH!

SECTOR 3599.
THE PLANET VORA.
WHERE ARE YOU?!? YOU'RE SCARING ME!
MAMA'S HERE! MAMA'S BACK!
EVERYTHING WILL BE ALL RIGHT NOW!
THERE'RE NO HEARTBEATS HERE, KRYB.
YOUR CHILDREN ARE GONE.
NO--IT'S NOT POSSIBLE--THEY WERE TOO YOUNG--THERE'RE NO TRANSPORTS OF ANY KIND HERE!
COME OUT FROM WHERE YOU'RE HIDING-- PLEASE TALK TO ME!
I'M SO SORRY FOR LEAVING YOU ALL ALONE!
WERE ALL THE CHILDREN BORN OF LANTERNS YOU THEN MURDERED?
YES--BUT I'VE NEVER HARMED ANY OF THE CHILDREN! I ADORE THEM--I DID WHAT I DID FOR THEIR WELL-BEING!
I GAVE THEM A HOME HERE--A PLANET ALL THEIR OWN TO THRIVE AND GROW ON!
I'VE SCANNED THE ENTIRE PLANET, KRYB.
THERE'RE ONLY TWO HEARTS BEATING RIGHT AT THIS MOMENT AND THEY BELONG TO US.
YOU HAVE TO HELP ME FIND THEM--I ALWAYS HEAR THEIR VOICES--NO MATTER HOW FAR--WHY CAN'T I HEAR THEM?!?
FAASH
I CAN'T GENERATE A HEART TETHER BECAUSE I'M NOT PICKING UP ANY HEARTBEATS--BUT THERE MAY BE ONE CHANCE...
...WHOEVER'S TAKEN THE CHILDREN HAS LEFT A RESIDUAL TRAIL OF SOME KIND, AND YOUR LOVE MAY HELP LIGHT THE WAY.

LANTERN MEDICAL INFIRMARY.
SUCH A VALIANT EFFORT, BUT MEANINGLESS.
IT'S NOW TIME TO GIVE THE CORPS YOUR ALL.
G-GET B-BACK...
FEAR.
WILL.
IT'S FITTING THAT YOU WILL ALL FEED THE CORPS YOU SO PROUDLY SERVED WITH YOUR LAST ACT AS LANTERNS.
FORFEITING NOT JUST YOUR LIFE, BUT YOUR EMOTIONAL ESSENCE AT ITS ZENITH.
AAGH!
YAGGH!
I DON'T KNOW WHAT THE HELL IS GOING ON...
ZZRAAAKK

...BUT GET YOUR DAMN HANDS OFF OF THEM!

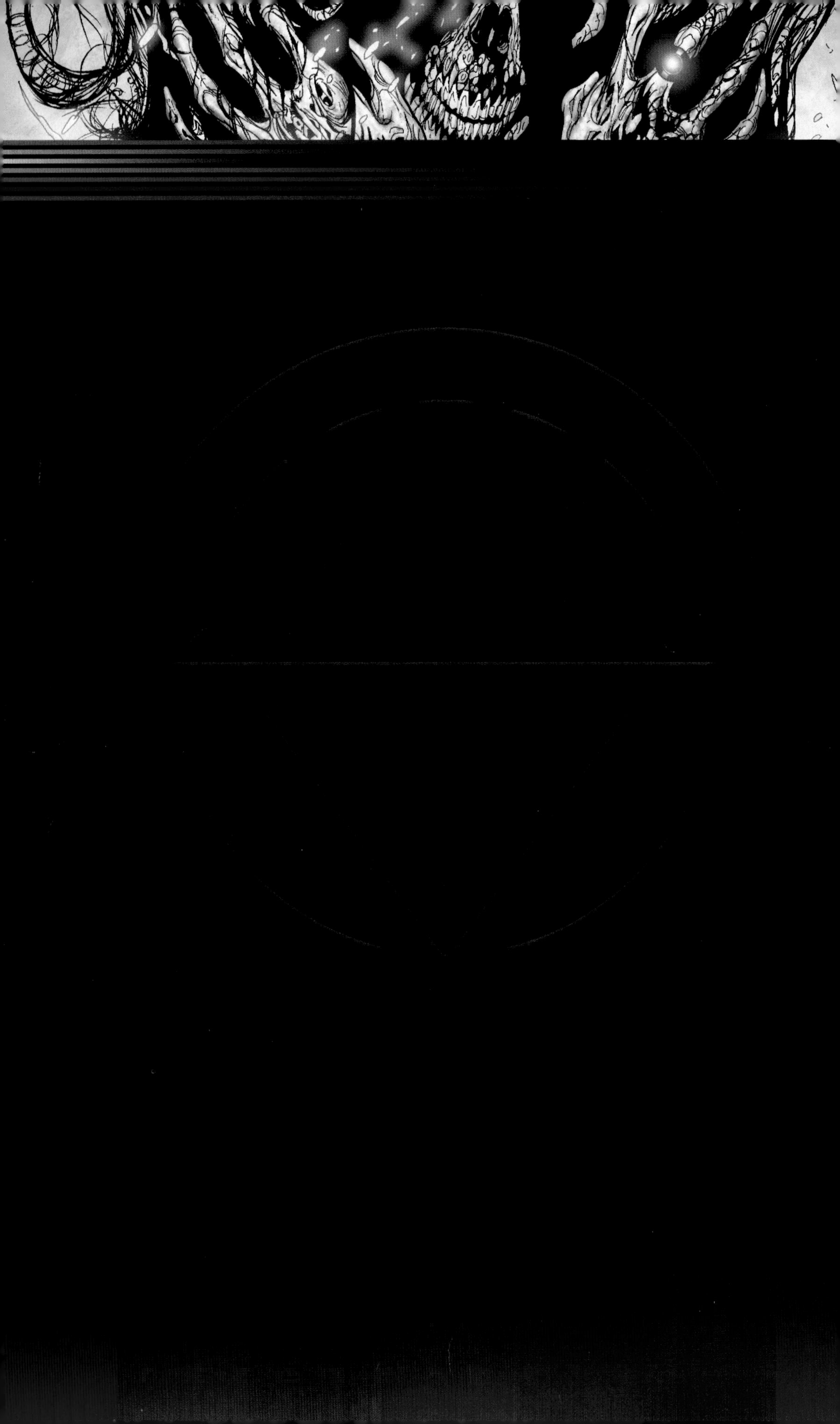

GREEN LANTERN CORPS 41
Cover by Patrick Gleason and Rebecca Buchman with Randy Mayor

HUNGRY HEART

PATRICK GLEASON
PENCILS

REBECCA BUCHMAN
KEITH CHAMPAGNE
TOM NGUYEN
INKS

OA
THE GREEN LANTERN INFIRMARY.
KEEP FIRING, IOLANDE!
DON'T LET THE ARMS REBUILD--
--TRY TO KEEP BURNING THEM BACK!
THEY'RE GENERATING TOO FAST, SORANIK!
I'M NOT SACRIFICING ANYBODY!
MAYBE I CAN FIND A WAY TO SURGICALLY REMOVE THE --
WILL.

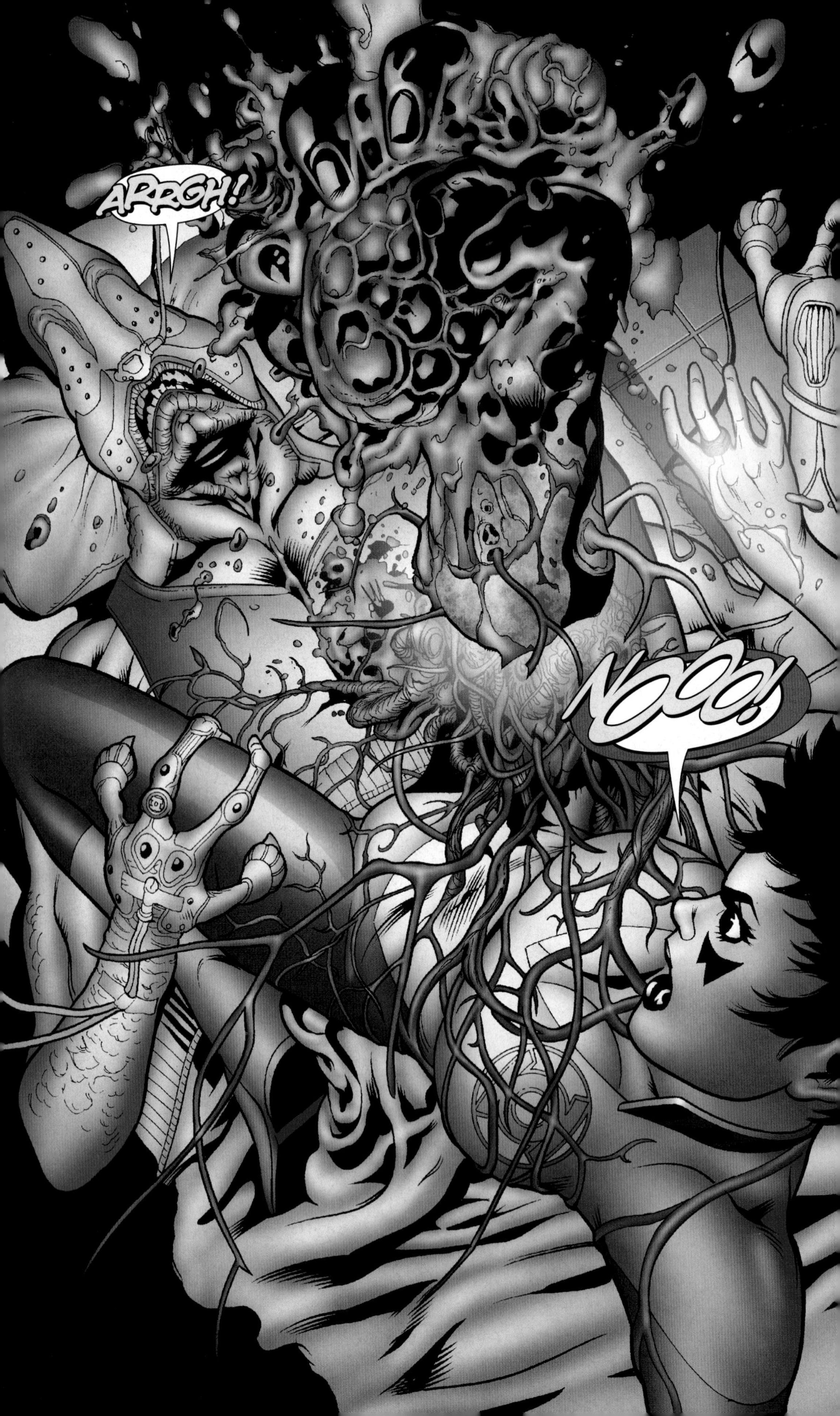
ARRGH!
NOOO!

WHAT THE--
POWER LEVELS 85.26%
AAAGH!
IT'S RE-FORMING ALL AROUND ME--I CAN'T GET IT OFF!
WILL.
RAGE.
FEAR.
DIVERT ALL POWER TO YOUR BODY SHIELD, NATU!
NOW!

SHRAZZAKKK
SHRIP
SHRIP
SHRIP
WATCH OUT!
BLACK RINGS ARE COMING THROUGH THE WALL!
FLESH.
FLESH.
FLESH.
FLESH.
FLESH.
FLESH.
FLESH.
RISE

ELSEWHERE ON OA.
AARRRGHH!
YOU THINK BECAUSE YOU AND JORDAN GOT ME AND THE OTHER LOST LANTERNS OFF OF BIOT THAT YOU'RE SOME KIND OF HERO?!?
YOU LEFT US THERE TO ROT FOR YEARS AT THE HANDS OF THE MANHUNTERS!
SKOOM
YOU COULD HAVE SAVED US LONG BEFORE JORDAN WAS FORCED BACK BY HIS GUILTY CONSCIENCE!
RRRRN!
KE'HAAN OL' PAL, I DON'T KNOW WHAT THESE DAMN BLACK RINGS ARE DOING TO YER CORPSES--
SHRAKK
--BUT I SWEAR TO GOD I'M GONNA FIND OUT--

--AND TOAST HIM GOOD!
YAARGHHH!
SHHOOOM
CRAPPITY CRAP CRAP...
...WE ARE IN FOR A WORLD OF FREAKIN' HURT.
FZZRAKK
GET BACK TO THE STARTING BLOCK, WHY DON'T YA?!?
SORRY TA BLAST AND RUN, YA EVIL HUNK A' JUNK, BUT I GOTTA PRIORITIZE AND GO SAVE SOME FELLOW LANTERNS WHO ARE STILL ALIVE AND KICKING!

...NO CHOICE, DAMN IT...THESE CREATURES LEAVE US NO CHOICE...
MAY THE GOD OF RANGRRA FORGIVE ME.
...LET US FIGHT, LANTERN NATU...WE CAN HELP...
SMASH!
NO, VOZ! I'VE STITCHED UP TOO MANY OF YOU TO LET YOU DIE ON YOUR BACKS HERE IN A HOSPITAL BED!
YOU CAN HELP US BY GETTING BETTER AND STRONGER SOMEWHERE ELSE!
COME ON!
WE HAVE TO PROTECT THE REST OF THE SICK AND WOUNDED BEFORE THESE THINGS PUT THEMSELVES BACK TOGETHER!
FOLLOW ME!
SOME-WHERE ELSE?!? WHAT KIND OF PLAN--
THEY'RE GOING ON A HEALING TRIP, IOLANDE!
IT'D BE HELPFUL IF I KNEW WHERE I WAS SENDING THEM!
THE ONLY PLACE I KNOW WHERE THEY'LL BE SAFE...

...MOGO.

WE'LL ESCORT THEM TO THE EDGE OF THE SECTOR AND--

KYLE...

...NO...
I'LL ESCORT TH WOUNDED. YOU GET DOWN--
I CAN'T LEAVE YOU ALONE TO--
GO.
NOW!

RAAAGH!
WILL.
RAGE.
HOW CAN SO MANY PEOPLE BE DEAD AND YOU'RE STILL ALIVE?
WHY DO YOU GET TO BURY EVERYONE, KYLE, AND NO ONE GETS TO BURY YOU?
AAGH!
I THINK IT'S TIME TO CHANGE ALL THAT.
IT'S TIME FOR YOU TO DIE, KYLE.
GET AWAY FROM HIM!
KYLE, ARE YOU ALL RIGHT?
THANKS TO YOU I AM.
LET'S GO FINISH THIS.

SKKRRKKRRKKRK
NO DOUBT ABOUT IT, LOVE IS IN THE--
KRAKOOM
I'D SAY THERE'S NOTHING IN THE AIR BUT THE SMELL OF THE ROTTEN CORPSE YOU'VE STOLEN.
LOVE.
RAGE.
WILL.
AND I WOULD SAY SOMEONE HERE IS MOTIVATED BY SOME PRETTY INTENSE FEELINGS TO PROTECT YOU..
YOU'VE GOT IT BAD, DON'T YOU, GIRL?

SHUT YOUR MOUTH, YOU DELUSIONAL WITCH.
I DON'T THINK SO.
THAT'S RUDE, KYLE.
NOW AREN'T YOU GOING TO INTRODUCE ME TO YOUR NEW GIRLFRIEND?
DID YOU TELL HER YOU'RE A LIAR?
SHUT UP.
I BET OUR HEARTBREAKER BOY TOLD YOU IT WAS YOUR SWEET LITTLE FACE HE SAW IN THE GLEAMING SAPPHIRE CRYSTAL.
KYLE, HOW DOES SHE KNOW ABOUT--
I'M JADE, THE LOVE OF HIS LIFE--I KNOW EVERYTHING ABOUT HIM. DO YOU?
HERE'S HOW IT ALWAYS ENDS, YOU KNOW, FOR KYLE'S GIRLS...
...IN A BOX, OR WORSE LIKE THE REST OF US.
I THOUGHT HE TOLD YOU--
--TO SHUT UP!

HIGH ABOVE OA.
FEAR.
WILL.
MOTHER--STOP--WHAT ARE YOU DOING?!
LOVE.
I BROUGHT YOUR BEATING HEART INTO THIS UNIVERSE, ARISIA...
...AND I WILL BE THE ONE TO TAKE THE FIRST BITE!
GET AWAY FROM ME!
ZZRRAAAPPP
YOU'VE ALWAYS BEEN SUCH AN EMOTIONAL GIRL, ARISIA.
YES, DON'T YOU SEE, YOU CAN FEED US AND JOIN US AT THE SAME TIME.
UNNN!
AND RIGHT NOW THAT'S A GOOD THING, DARLING.
BUT ALL THIS FLYING AWA FROM US--IT HURTING OU FEELINGS...

SKOOM
...THIS IS SIMPLY NO WAY TO BEGIN A FAMILY REUNION!
DETECTING LANTERN ARISIA FROM SECTOR 2815.
THANK YOU FOR VISITING THE HALL OF LANTERNS TODAY.
HERE ARE THE LANTERNS WHO HAVE SO PROUDLY SERVED OUR SECTOR OVER THE MANY YEARS.
RAAAGH!
LANTERN TARA RRAB. DECEASED.
LANTERN FENTARA RRAB. DECEASED.
LANTERN MARATA RRAB. DECEASED.
LANTERN ARISIA RRAB. ACTIVE.
YOU WANT A FAMILY REUNION...

...I'LL GIVE YOU A FAMILY REUNION!
THE RRABS HAVE SERVED THE CORPS FOR HUNDREDS OF YEARS...
...AND WE DON'T LIKE SEEING OUR *LEGACY* SCREWED WITH!

IS THIS HOW YOU REPAY A FATHER'S LOVE?!?
YOU USE ALL THE LANTERN SKILLS AND KNOWLEDGE I TAUGHT YOU AGAINST ME?!?

I HAD HOPED TO HAVE A DAUGHTER WHO WOULD BUILD ON MY ACHIEVEMENTS AS A LANTERN AND EARN THE RESPECT AND HONOR OF THE GUARDIANS.
YOU WERE OUR CHANCE AT IMMORTALITY, OF CONTINUING THE PROUD TRADITION OF SERVICE.
BUT YOU'VE BEEN NOTHING BUT A DISAPPOINTMENT, ARISIA.

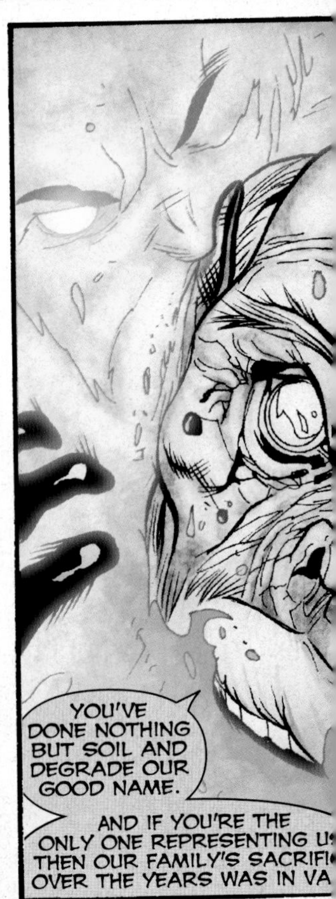
YOU'VE DONE NOTHING BUT SOIL AND DEGRADE OUR GOOD NAME.
AND IF YOU'RE THE ONLY ONE REPRESENTING U THEN OUR FAMILY'S SACRIFI OVER THE YEARS WAS IN VA

YOU'RE ALL JUST BLACK HOLES SENT BY SOMEONE BENT ON DESTROYING THE CORPS!
AND YOU'RE NOT SUCKING ME IN!
I THINK IT'S TIME FOR THAT **GROUP HUG** AFTER ALL!
I WILL **NEVER** DISHONOR THE RRAB NAME OR THE CORPS...
...FOR AS LONG AS I LIVE AND WEAR THIS RING.

ELSEWHERE ON OA.
KEEP THE FORMATION TIGHT!
FULL POWER, POOZERS!
THESE THINGS ARE US!
HOW CAN WE FIRE AT OUR OWN--
SCRAP THAT OF YOUR HEA NOW! THES THINGS ARE N OUR HONOR DEAD!

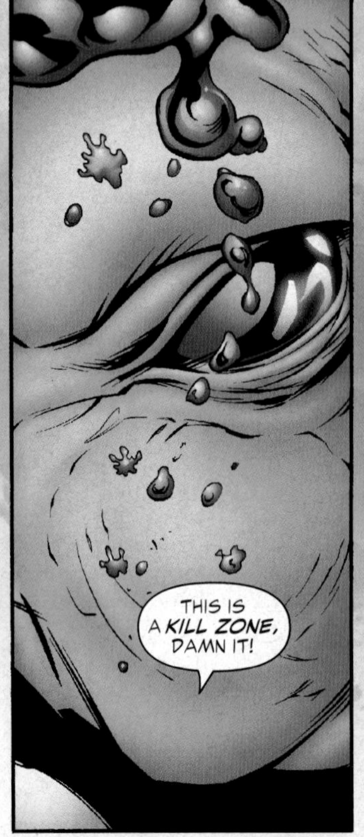

THIS IS A **KILL ZONE,** DAMN IT!

THAT MEANS KILL OR BE KILL**AAAARGH!**

UGNN.
NO.
NO!
HEY, POOZER!
YOUR TRAINING OF LANTERN ROOKIES HAS BEEN PISS POOR, BRILLOLOG!
GUESS YOU DIDN'T BELONG IN MY CORPS AFTER ALL.
LANTERN ERMEY!

YOU'RE A LEGEND! YOU TRAINED THOUSANDS OF LANTERNS TO BE THE BEST!
YOU TRAINED ME!
GUESS I DIDN'T DO THAT GOOD A JOB, HUH?
HERE, I THINK THESE ROOKIES BELONG TO YOU!
YOU'RE DEAD! YOU DIED IN MY ARMS!
I CARRIED YOU BACK TO OA MYSELF!
THAT'S FUNNY, I DON'T FEEL DEAD!
BUT COME TO THINK OF IT, I DO REMEMBER YOU HANGING ME OUT TO DRY.
TOOK YOUR SWEET TIME COMING IN AS BACKUP, AND I TOOK ONE IN THE BACK 'CAUSE OF IT.
I WAS JUST FOLLOWING YOUR OWN DAMN ORDERS!
A GOOD LANTERN--A TRUE LANTERN--WOULD'VE READ THE SITUATION BETTER AND PROVIDED COVERING FIRE.
YOU DID NEITHER.
I GOT THERE AND--
YOU GOT NOWHERE. YOU COST ME MY LIFE--YOU MIGHT AS WELL HAVE BEEN THE ONE TO PULL THE TRIGGER AND KILL ME YOURSELF!

I SAVED ALL THE LANTERNS AND THE CIVILIANS!
BUT YOU LEFT OUT ONE LITTLE DETAIL.
I DID MY JOB--I DID MY DUTY!
YEAH, YOU SURE DID. YOU SAVED SINESTRO.
HE WAS A LANTERN! HE WAS ONE OF THE--
YOU SAVED THE SCOURGE OF THE GREEN LANTERN CORPS AND THE UNIVERSE ITSELF. NICE JOB.
HELL, YOU'RE REALLY RESPONSIBLE FOR THE DEATH OF THOUSANDS AND THOUSANDS OF BEINGS, AREN'T YOU?
SHUT UP!
YOU REEK OF DEATH, BRILLOLOG.
AND WHEN WORD GETS OUT HOW YOU LET THE ROOKIES GET SLAUGHTERED HERE TODAY--
--NO ONE WILL EVER WANT TO BE A LANTERN AGAIN.
I SAID--
SHUT UP!
POWER RINGS WILL BE TURNED AWAY IN DROVES, AND MY OLD CORPS WILL BE WIPED AWAY FOREVER.
OA WILL BE A GHOST TOWN THANKS TO YOU, BRILLOLOG FROM THE PLANET OF BALLOWAX!

SAY IT, ERMEY!
SKRUNCH
MY
FNAM
NAME
FOOM
IS
KILOWOG!
FOOM FOOM
IF YOU'RE TRYING TO PULVERIZE MY HEART, YOU'RE DOING A NICE JOB--YOU CAN HAVE IT.
I'LL FIND MYSELF--
SKOOOM
--ANOTHER ONE!
AARRGH!

BRATTA BRATTA BRATTA
KEEP THE PERIMETER TIGHT, ISAMOT!
DON'T GIVE THESE BLACK LANTERNS AN INCH!
NO $#%& KIDDING!
POOM POOM POOM
HEY VATH, HEY ISAMOT!
YOU DON'T LOOK TOO HAPPY TO SEE YOUR OLD PALS TANAKATA Z AND QUOND!
BUT I GUESS WHY WOULD YOU, SINCE YOU LET US GET BUTCHERED IN OUR OWN SECTOR HOUSE!
ZZRAAAKKK
...WHAT THE HELL... A BUNCHA KIDS...?
HNNN.
I CAN TASTE THEIR HEARTS FROM HERE.

THEIR *WILLPOWER* IS MAKING MY TUMMY GRUMBLE.
I'M REALLY HUNGRY.
WE WANNA EAT--
--AND WE WANNA EAT NOW!
RRRNN!
YUM YUM EAT HIM UP!
ARHHH!

NRRR--LIGHT BRIGHT--BRIGHT LIGHT!
WHAT THE HELL--
REK LO KLEK!
FAASSH
I FEEL YOUR PAIN, GREEN LANTERNS.
THESE VIAL ABOMINATIONS MUST NOW FEEL THEIR OWN.

GREEN LANTERN CORPS 42
Cover by Patrick Gleason and Rebecca Buchman with Randy Mayor

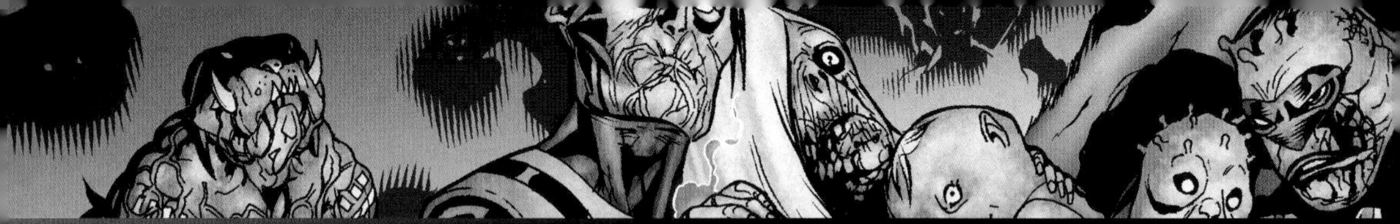

SACRIFICE OF WILL

PATRICK GLEASON
PENCILS

REBECCA BUCHMAN
TOM NGUYEN
INKS

DR.
AND JUST WHO THE HELL ARE YOU?!?
YOU CAN CALL ME MUNK.
MY TRIBE PRESERVES THE INDIGO LIGHT OF COMPASSION.
A SECOND AGO YOU WERE TALKING ABOUT ALL THIS "HELP" YOU WERE POPPING IN HERE TO BRING!
"COMPASSION" IS THE ONE THING WE DON'T NEED AT THE MOMENT!
MAMA, CAN I EAT THE LANTERN'S HEART NOW?
OF COURSE MY DARLING. PATIENCE. ALL IN DUE TIME.
WHAT DID I MISS, VATH?
I AM HERE TO TELL YOU THAT ALL THE LANTERN HOMEWORLDS ARE UNDER A FULL-SCALE ATTACK BY THE BLACK LANTERNS.
ZAMARON, THE BASTION OF LOVE AND VIOLET, IS GONE-- THEIR CENTRAL POWER BATTERY HAS BEEN DESTROYED.
AND IF WE DO NOT STOP THE BLACK LANTERNS HERE...

...OA AND THE GREEN LANTERN CORPS CENTRAL POWER BATTERY WILL BE THE NEXT TO FALL!

THEY DON'T SEEM TOO CONCERNED ABOUT THE CENTRAL BATTERY TO ME RIGHT NOW!
RING--WHO THE HELL ARE THESE KILLER KIDS?!?
DNA SCANNING CONFIRMS THAT THESE ARE THE CHILDREN OF LANTERNS MURDERED BY THE SINESTRO CORPS MEMBER KRYB.
ALL THESE... CORPHANS AND BLACK LANTERNS WANT TO DO IS RIP OUR HEARTS OUT AND KILL AS MANY OF US AS POSSIBLE!
WE OF THE INDIGO TRIBE BELIEVE THAT IT IS ONLY ONE PART OF THEIR PLAN.
WITH EACH EMOTION-FILLED HEART THEY CONSUME, THEIR RINGS SERVE TO CHANNEL THIS EMOTIONAL ENERGY AND SEND IT ELSEWHERE...
WILL.
...WHILE AT THE SAME TIME THEY'RE BUILDING THE SEMBLANCE OF A CORPS WITH ANOTHER PARTICULAR MISSION IN MIND.
AAIIEEEE!
CONNECTION SEVERED.
WITH EACH DEATH THEIR NUMBERS GROW--CAUSING A NEW BLACK LANTERN TO RISE--
--INCREASING THEIR FORCES AND THEIR CHANCES TO COMBAT THE GREEN LANTERNS THAT WILL DEFEND THE BATTERY.

CONNECTION SEVERED.
CONNECTION SEVERED.
CONNECTION SEVERED.
FAASSH
AAIIEEEEE!
AAIIEEEEE!
CONNECTION SEVERED.
AAIIEEEEE!
I HOPE THAT WALKING STICK OF YOURS CAN DO MORE TRICKS LIKE THAT--
FEED US! FEED US! FEED US!
BRATTA BRATTA BRATTA
FEED US! FEED US! FEED US!
--BECAUSE THAT'S 8 DOWN AND 40 MORE TO GO AND WE'RE GOING TO NEED ALL THE FIREPOWER WE CAN GET!
FEED US! FEED US! FEED US!
FEED US! FEED US! FEED US!

YOU TRANSPORTED IN, MUNK--TRANSPORT US OUT--
--GET US TO A BETTER DEFILADE POSITION SO WE'RE NOT SURROUNDED AND WE CAN ZERO IN ON THESE BASTARDS!
CONNECTION SEVERED.
CONNECTION SEVERED.
AAIIEEEE!
CONNECTION SEVERED.
SPATIAL LEAPS UTILIZE TOO MUCH ENERGY. IT DRAWS A SIGNIFICANT AMOUNT OF POWER AWAY FROM MY RING AND IT WOULD PREVENT ME FROM NEUTRALIZING AS MANY OF THESE BLACK LANTERNS AS WE CAN.
CONNECTION SEVERED.
AAIIEEEE!
HOW ARE YOU ZAPPING THEM AND WE CAN'T?!?
THE SIMPLE EXPLANATION IS THAT BY MERGING OUR INDIGO LIGHT OF COMPASSION WITH THE GREEN RADIANCE OF WILLPOWER WE CAN DESTROY A BLACK LANTERN AND THEIR POWER RING.
GREAT, THEN LET'S THROW UP A MIRROR CONSTRUCT AND WE CAN SATURATE THE ENTIRE PLANET WITH --
OUR ABILITY TO RENDER THEM POWERLESS ONLY COMES FROM DIRECT AND INTIMATE DISCHARGES.
AN EXPANSIVE ATTACK--A BROADENING OF THE LIGHTS--WOULD DILUTE THEIR LUMINOSITY AND RENDER THEM INERT.
THIS LOOKS "INERT" TO ME.
OR THEY'RE JUST CATCHING THEIR BREATH.
WISHFUL THINKING.
100% POWER LEVEL EXCEEDED.
DEVOUR WILL.
100% POWER LEVEL EXCEEDED.
DEVOUR WILL.
100% POWER LEVEL EXCEEDED.
DEVOUR WILL.

ELSEWHERE ON OA.
AARRGH!

WHAT ARE YOU SCREAMING FOR, BRILLOLOG?
IF I WERE YOU I'D BE LOOKING FORWARD TO THE BLACKNESS.

AARRGH!
YOU'VE FAILED EVERYONE.
YOUR PEOPLE.
YOUR CORPS.
THE ROOKIES.
YOURSELF.

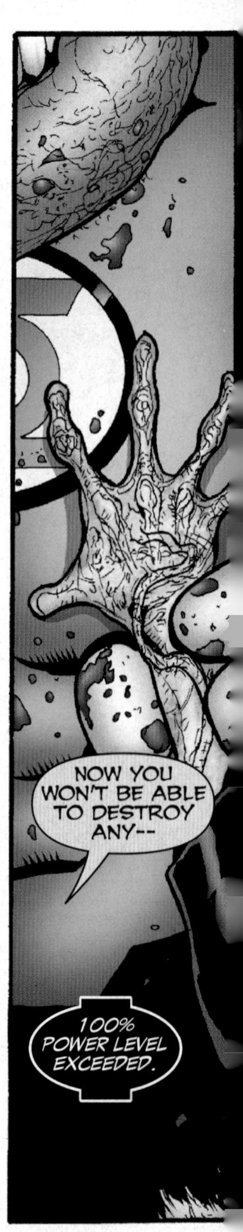
NOW YOU WON'T BE ABLE TO DESTROY ANY--
100% POWER LEVEL EXCEEDED.

RRNNN.
DEVOUR WILL.

WHAT ARE YOU STARING AT?!?!
YOU ALL KNEW THE RISKS WHEN YOU ACCEPTED THE RING!
100% POWER LEVEL EXCEEDED.
DEVOUR WILL.
100% POWER LEVEL EXCEEDED.
DEVOUR WILL.
DEVOUR WILL.
I NEVER HID THE FACT THAT DEATH WAS A PART OF THE CORPS!
I DRILLED IT INTO YOUR HEADS--YOU KNEW THE HISTORY--YOU KNEW SACRIFICES ARE MADE!
DEVOUR WILL.
DEVOUR WILL.
DEVOUR WILL.
EVERYONE ALWAYS THINKS THEY'RE IMMUNE FROM IT--THAT IT'LL BE THE LANTERN NEXT TO HIM!
WELL, IT WAS YOU!
AND YOU!
DEVOUR WILL.
DEVOUR WILL.
AND YOU!
AND YOU!
ALL OF YOU!
DID YOU THINK YOU WERE SPECIAL--
--THAT YOUR NAMES WOULD NEVER BE INSCRIBED IN THE LANTERN CRYPT?!?
DEVOUR WILL.
DEVOUR WILL.
YOU WERE ALL LANTERNS!
AND LANTERNS DIE...
...LANTERNS DIE...

RGGR!
RRRN.
DID YOU REALLY THINK YOU COULD SCARE ME WITH THAT PUPPET LIGHT SHOW OF YOURS?
I'VE SEEN PLENTY OF DEATH.
AND IF YOU THINK I'M GOING TO LET SOME ABOMINATION LIKE YOU DESTROY WHAT I HAVE--
WHAT WAS THAT?
YOU'RE GOING TO HAVE TO SPEAK UP, I CAN'T HEAR YOU WITH MY FIST SHOVED IN YOUR MOUTH.
WHAT WE HAVE.
100% POWER LEVEL EXCEEDED.
DEVOUR WILL.
KYLE--
WHAT?!?
SORANIK!

THIS IS CRAZY!
THE BLACK LANTERN WAS BENT ON KILLING US A SECOND AGO--
NOW IT'S ACTING LIKE WE DON'T EVEN EXIST!
DIVERT ALL POWER TO YOUR RING--I DON'T WANT TO BLOW YOUR HAND OFF!
DEVOUR WILL.
ZZZRRRAKKK
WHERE THE HELL IS--
--IT GOING?

DEVOUR WILL.

OKAY, WE'RE DYING WITH OUR BOOTS ON, PEOPLE...
...AND WE'RE DYING STANDING UP!
NOT IN OUR HOUSE!
NOT TODAY!
POUR IT ON!

DEVOUR WILL.
DEVOUR WILL.
DEVOUR WILL.
DEVOUR WILL.
THE OBJECTIVE OF THE BLACK LANTERNS HAS CHANGED!
THEY ARE SEEKING TO DESTROY THE BATTERY AND EXTINGUISH ITS LIGHT!
CEASE AND DESIST FROM ALL CURRENT BATTLE STATIONS AND REPORT TO THE CENTRAL POWER BATTERY FOR DEFENSIVE ACTION!
REPEAT, ALL LANTERNS REPORT TO THE CENTRAL POWER BATTERY FOR DEFENSIVE ACTION!
SO WHAT COLORED CRAYOLA LANTERN ARE YOU, BUDDY--DEEP PURPLE?!?
I AM FROM THE INDIGO TRIBE, GREEN LANTERN, AND IF WE CAN--
YEAH, WHATEVER--WORKS FOR ME--I AIN'T LOOKING NO GIFT HORSE IN THE MOUTH!
CONNECTION SEVERED.
AAIIEEEE!
AAIIEEEE!
CONSTRUCT DARK MATTER.
WITH YOUR HELP, INDIGO MAN, WE CAN FINALLY PUT SOME HURT ON THESE COCKROACHES AND STOP 'EM FROM PUTTIN' THEMSELVES--

"--BACK TOGETHER."

BATTERY FOUNDATION COMPROMISED.

THIS AIN'T LOOKING GOOD!
GONNA BE LEAVING A LOT OF BLOOD ON THE FLOOR ON THIS ONE, KYLE!
GOD HELP US, I THINK YOU'RE RIGHT, GUY.

UNFF!
C'MON!
I'VE GOT AN IDEA!

LET'S ADDRESS THE SOURCE OF THIS HIDEOUS CONSTRUCT, LANTERN!
YES, LET'S!

SALAAK, RELEASE SCIENCELL 8985!
LANTERN RAYNER! WHAT ARE YOU DOING IN THE--
JUST DO IT, SALAAK!
THIS DAMN GIANT CONSTRUCT IS TRYING TO PULL THE CENTRAL POWER BATTERY OUT OF THE GROUND!
CUT ITS FREAKIN' HANDS OFF!
WE'RE WORKING ON THE LEFT ONE, VATH!
SORANIK-- GRAB OUR NEW LANTERN BUDDY AND GET THE HELL OUT OF THERE!
BUT, KYLE, WITH HIS HELP WE MAY BE ABLE TO--
OUT! NOW!
OKAY, WE'RE OUT!

DEVOUR WILL.
DEVOUR WILL.
DEVOUR W--
PUTTING VICE BACK INTO HIS JACK-IN-THE BOX'S NOT GONNA BE A CAKEWALK, OL' BUDDY!
LET'S WORRY ABOUT ONE THING AT A TIME, GUY!
FOOM
HERE YOU GO, SUCKERS-- DON'T SAY WE NEVER GAVE YA ANYTHING!
RRRAAAARRRGHH!

LET'S GET OUT OF THE RED LANTERN'S SIGHT-LINE SO HE CAN TAKE APART THE BLACK LANTERNS GENERATING THIS CONSTRUCT WITHOUT GETTING DISTRACTED BY US!
YEAH, HE CAN ALWAYS TRY AND KILL US LATER...
...ONCE HE RUNS OUTTA BLACK LANTERNS!
BY AUTHORITY OF THE GUARDIANS, YOU FORFEIT YOUR EXISTENCE, RED LANTERN VICE.
NO PRISONER ESCAPES THE SCIENCELLS.

IT'S WORKING! THE BATTERY IS LOSING ALTITUDE!
THE RED LANTERN'S DAMAGING THE BLACK LANTERNS' BODIES AT SUCH A FAST PACE THAT THEY CAN'T GENERATE ENOUGH POWER TO MAINTAIN THE CONSTRUCT!
AARGH!
RAARGH--!
CRAP! THE BLACK LANTERN CONSTRUCT'S GETTING BRIGHTER!
AND THE DAMN BATTERY'S GETTING HIGHER AND HIGHER AGAIN!
LET'S PLAY WITH THE SHINY BALL.
BATTERY PRESENT.
BATTERY PRESENT.
DEVOUR WILL.
DEVOUR WILL.

NEGATIVE, LANTERN SALAAK.
THE ALPHA LANTERNS ARE THE ONLY ONES CAPABLE OF RECTIFYING THIS SITUATION AND PRESERVING THE CENTRAL BATTERY.
DEVOUR WILL.
WHAT MAKES YOU SO SHINY?
DO YOU HAVE A TOY FOR ME?
LANTERN CHASELON!
FALL BACK IMMEDIATELY--YOUR INTERNAL POWER BATTERY IS IN DANGER OF BEING BREACHED!
THE POSSIBILITY OF MY POWER BATTERY BEING DESTROYED, LANTERN SALAAK, IS--
RAAGGH!
DEVOUR WILL.
DEVOUR WILL.
DEVOUR WILL.
SHRRRIPPP
RED LANTERN VICE AND ALPHA LANTERN CHASELON HAVE BOTH BEEN COMPROMISED, RAYNER.
UPLOADS I AM RECEIVING INDICATE A SMALL FISSURE IS IN DANGER OF RUPTURING ON THE ALPHA BATTERY.
NEED I REMIND YOU AN ALPHA BATTERY THAT THE GUARDIANS PLACED INSIDE IS--
UNDERSTOOD, SALAAK--

WILL.
--I'M ON MY WAY!
DEVOUR WILL.
DEVOUR WILL.

THANKS FOR THE HANDOFF!
DEVOUR WILL.
DEVOUR WILL.
DEVOUR WILL.
DEVOUR WILL.
DEVOUR WILL.

DEVOUR WILL.
NOW GET ALL YOUR DEAD ASSES OVER HERE...
DEVOUR WILL.
DEVOUR WILL.

...SO I CAN TAKE AS MANY...

...OF YOU WITH ME!

AND DON'T WORRY, NO ONE'S LEAVING MY PARTY EARLY!
ENERGY DOME CREATED.
DEVOUR WILL.
ALPHA LANTERN BATTERY DETONATION IMMINENT.
DEVOUR WILL.
I LOVE YOU, SORANIK.
WHAT?
KYLE, WHERE ARE--
AND YOU TOO, GUY.
YOU'VE BEEN LIKE A BROTHER TO

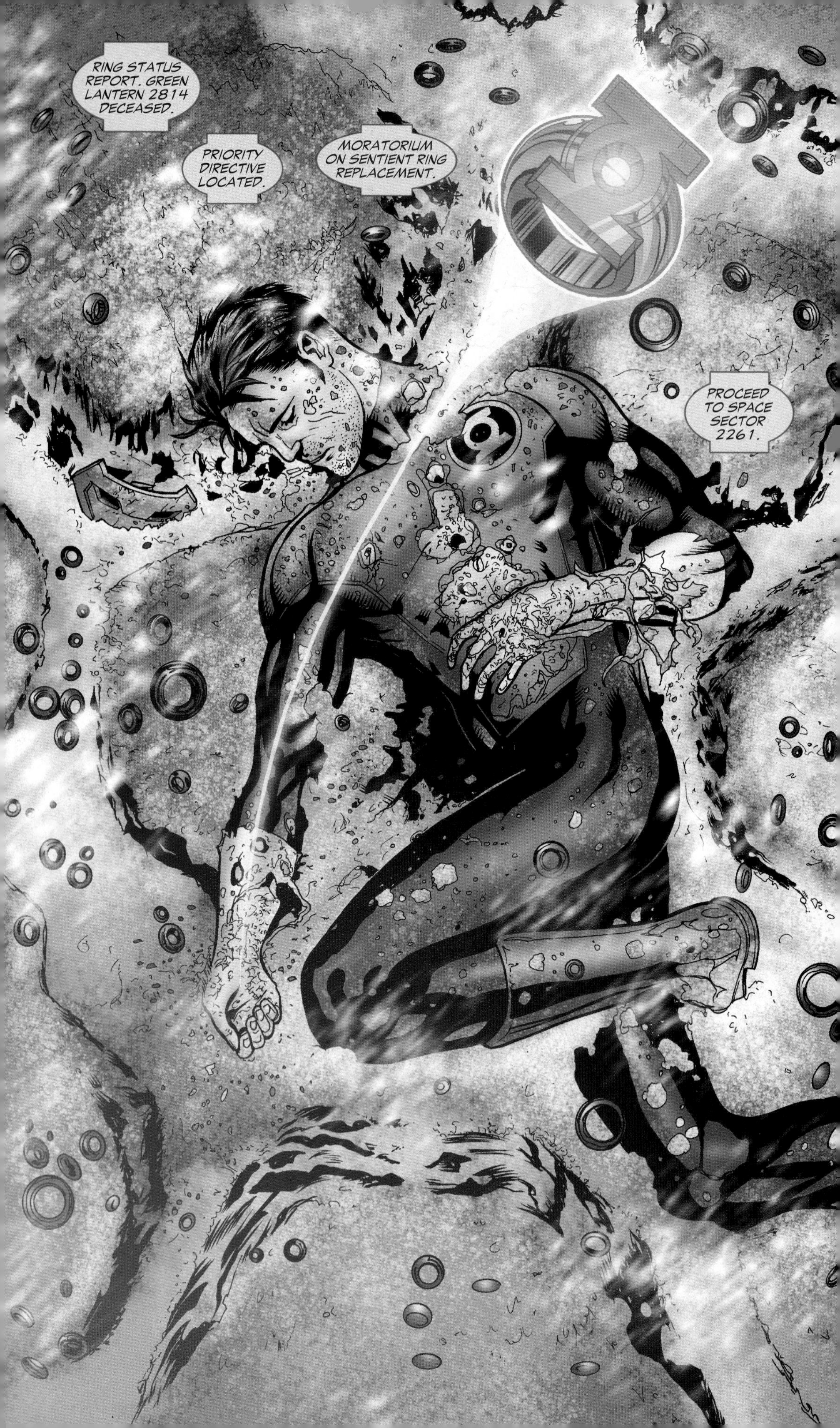
RING STATUS REPORT. GREEN LANTERN 2814 DECEASED.
PRIORITY DIRECTIVE LOCATED.
MORATORIUM ON SENTIENT RING REPLACEMENT.
PROCEED TO SPACE SECTOR 2261.

GREEN LANTERN CORPS 43
Cover by Patrick Gleason and Rebecca Buchman with Randy Mayor

RED BADGE OF RAGE
PART ONE

PATRICK GLEASON
PENCILS

REBECCA BUCHMAN
TOM NGUYEN
PATRICK GLEASON
INKS

KYLE!
NO!
RING STATUS REPORT. GREEN LANTERN 2814 HONOR GUARD DECEASED.

PRIORITY DIRECTIVE LOCATED.
MORATORIUM ON SENTIENT RING REPLACEMENT.
PROCEED TO LANTERN MOGO IN SPACE SECTOR 2261.
YOU'RE NOT GOIN' ANYWHERE--
--BUT BACK ON KYLE'S FINGER!
OMIGOD-- KYLE--PLEASE DON'T LEAVE ME--
CONTROL YOURSELF, DAMN IT! FOCUS!
YOU'RE A SURGEON-- YOU SAVE PEOPLE--
--NOW SAVE THE MAN YOU LOVE!
PROCEED TO SPACE SECTOR 2261.
KLANK
SHUT THE HELL UP!
YOU'RE KYLE'S RING!
NO ONE ELSE'S

PROCEED TO SPACE SECTOR 2261.
RRNNN!
HE'S EARNED THAT RING MORE THAN ANYBODY FER CRISSAKES!
YOU'RE NOT TAKING IT AWAY FROM HIM!
PROCEED TO SPACE SECTOR 2261.
RRGGN!
YOU CAN'T TAKE IT AWAY!
HE'S ALIVE-- YOU'LL SEE-- HE'S--
FWOOM
SKLANG
COME BACK TO ME, KYLE!
FIGHT IT!
--DEAD--
...YOU KILLED HIM...
GUY GARDNER OF SPACE SECTOR 2814.
YOU HAVE GREAT RAGE IN YOUR HEART.
YOU BASTARDS KILLED HIM!

WELCOME TO THE RED LANTERN CORPS.
HHHRRKKKK!
AND NOW I'M GONNA KILL ALL OF YOU!
BARIIM BARIIM BABUM

AAAARRRGHH!
GUY! NO! DON'T LET IT CONTROL YOU!
KYLE WOULDN'T WANT THIS!
YARRGHH!
BUT I DO!
CONNECTION SEVERED.
CONNECTION SEVERED.

CONNECTION SEVERED.
RRRAGGHH!
DEVOUR WILL.
DEVOUR WILL.
B BBB BBBBRRRB
BLARGHHHH!
SHUNK SHUNK SHUNK SHUNK
KYLLEEEE

C'MON, KYLE, DON'T GIVE UP ON ME NOW!
YOUR HEART WANTS TO START!
LET IT!
ZZZRAKK
KYLE RAYNER OF--
--EARTH.
GET AWAY FROM HIM!
ZZZRAK

KYLE RAYNER OF--
YOU CAN'T HAVE HIM!

YOU WON'T HAVE HIM!
KYLE RAYNER--
NO!

--OF EARTH.
OFF! GET OFF!

IT'S NOT HIS TIME!
RIS--
FAASH

CONNECTION SEVERED.
IT IS EVERYONE'S TIME, LANTERN...

...AND IT IS NO ONE'S TIME.
CKRAK

BUT YOU D NOT HAVE MUCH TIM TO BRING THIS LANTE BACK BEFO ANOTHER BLACK RIN SEEKS TO-
HRRM

KYLE
AYNER OF
EARTH.
I WAS MISTAKEN.
YOU HAVE NO TIME WHATSOEVER.
CONNECTION SEVERED.
CONNECTION SEVERED.
CONNECTION SEVERED.
I WILL DO ALL THAT I CAN TO DEFEND YOU, YOUNG LANTERN!
CONNECTION SEVERED.
ONNECTION SEVERED.
AND SO WILL WE!
CONNECTION SEVERED.
CONNECTION SEVERED.
CONNECTION SEVERED.

ELSEWHERE ON OA.
NO...
I TOLD YOU BEFORE, THERE WERE NO HEARTBEATS TO FOLLOW, KRYB.
THERE'S NO SIGN OF LIFE COMING FROM THOSE POOR CHILDREN--WE WERE LUCKY TO FIND THEM AT ALL HERE IN THE MIDDLE OF ALL THIS.
EAT THE GREEN.
THEY'RE MOVING-- THEY'RE FLYING--
EAT THE GREEN.
...THIS MUST BE A MISTAKE, SAPPHIRE.
THEY CAN'T BE DEAD.
EAT THE GREEN.
THEY'RE UNDEAD.
THEY'RE NOT THE CHILDREN YOU STOLE-- NOT THE CHILDREN YOU LEFT TO DIE ON YOUR DESOLATE PLANET.

I WAS STOLEN FROM THEM!
YOU AND YOUR KIND KEPT ME LOCKED IN THAT DAMNED CRYSTAL!
GAKK!
YOU HELPED KILL MY BABIES!
FZZRAKK
YAAGH!
THEY WERE NEVER YOUR BABIES TO BEGIN WITH, KRYB!
AND I SHOULD'VE KNOWN YOU'D NEVER KEEP YOUR PROMISE TO RETURN TO ZAMARON!

YOU PROMISED YOU'D HELP ME SAVE THEM!
THERE ARE NO CHILDREN LEFT TO SAVE.
STAR SAPPHIRE MIRI. THE HEART IS BEING ATTACKED IN SECTOR ZERO.
DEATH LOOKS TO EXTINGUISH ETERNAL LOVE.
YOU'LL REMAIN HERE WHILE I HELP THE LANTERNS FIGHT THESE--
AAHH!
TAKE ME THERE.
NOW.
THREE HEARTS ATTUNED.
YOU CAN'T LEAVE ME LIKE THIS!
WHO WILL SAVE MY BABIES?!?
TETHER TARGETED.

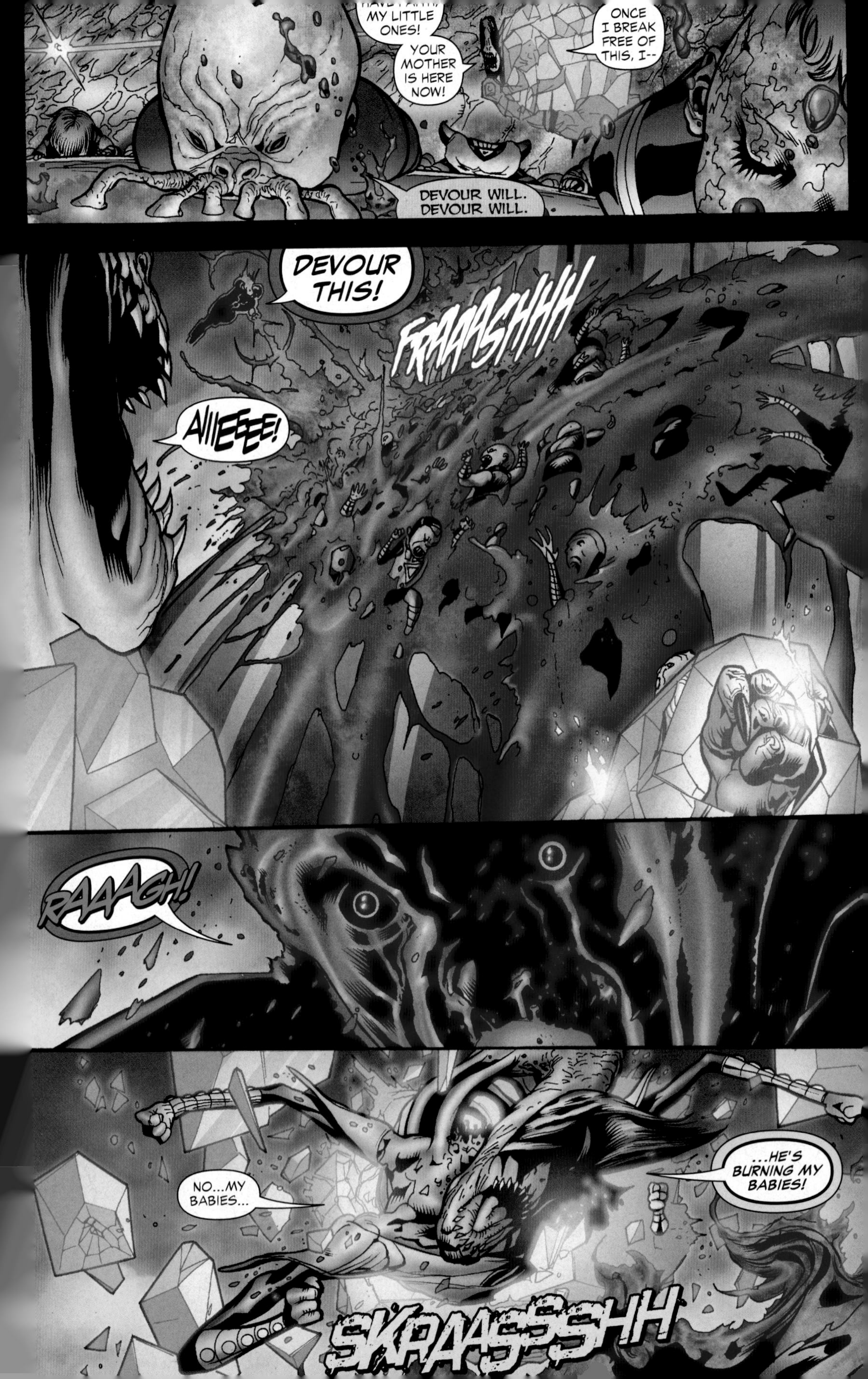

MY LITTLE ONES!
YOUR MOTHER IS HERE NOW!
ONCE I BREAK FREE OF THIS, I--
DEVOUR WILL. DEVOUR WILL.
DEVOUR THIS!
FRAAASHHH
AIIIEEEE!
RAAAGH!
NO...MY BABIES...
...HE'S BURNING MY BABIES!
SKRAASSSHH

GET AWAY FROM MY CHILDREN, YOU MONSTER!
SKOOM
RRNNN!
YARRGHH!
SHUNK
CHOKE ON IT!
RRAAGGHH!
SHRRIPP
AIIIEEEEE!
GAKK!

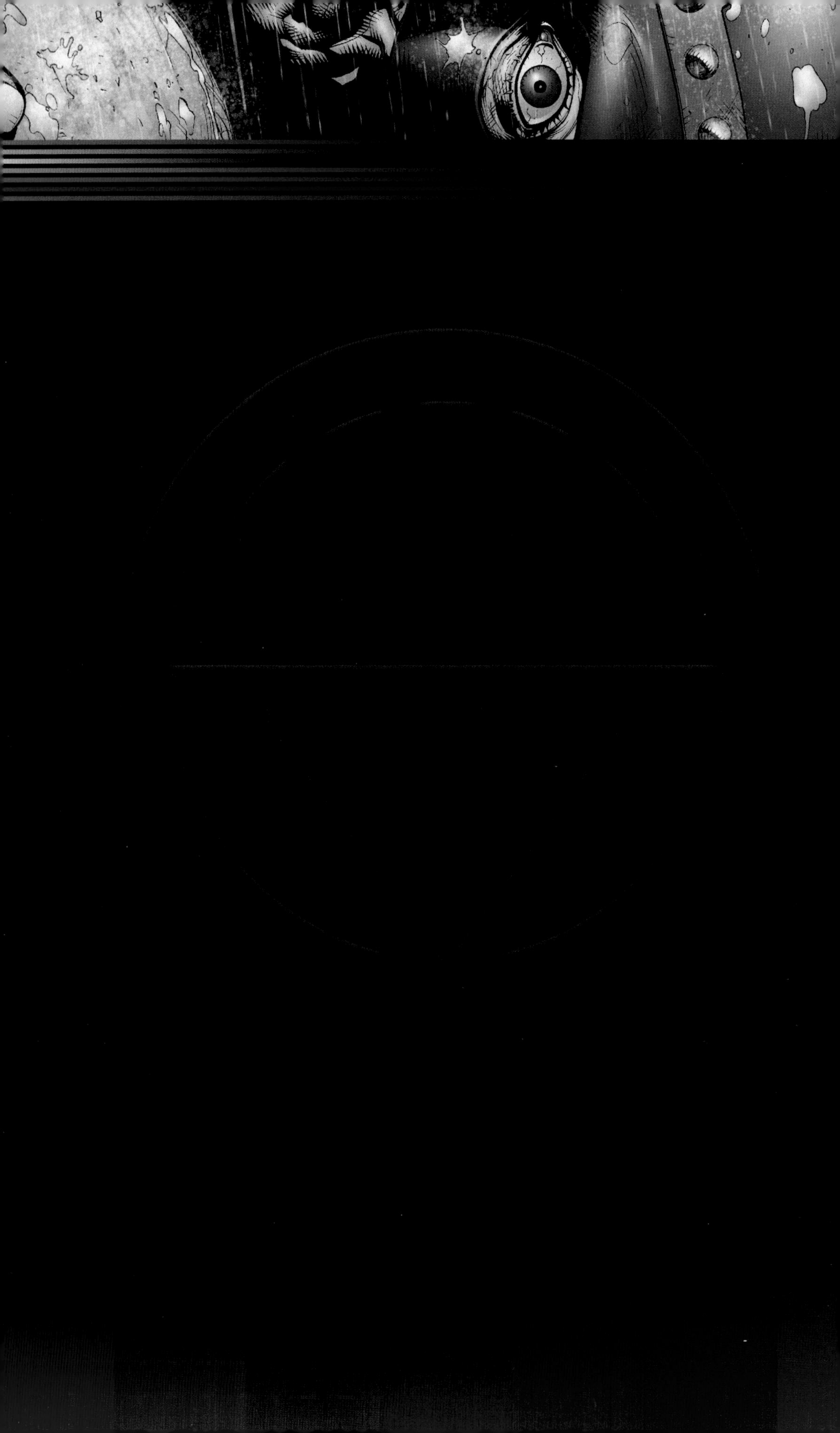

C'MON! C'MON!
YOUR FRIENDS ARE HERE GIVING US TIME!
AAGGHH!
NOW FIGHT, DAMN--
TETHER TARGETED.
HEARTBREAK LOCATED.
WHAT THE HELL--
NO-- HOLD YOUR FIRE!
YOUR DYING LOVE HAS CALLED ME HERE, LANTERN.
PLEASE... CAN YOU HELP HIM...
...HELP US...

CONNECTION SEVERED.
HIS HEART'S STOPPED--WE DON'T HAVE MUCH--
I MET YOU BOTH BEFORE WHEN YOU DELIVERED THAT BEAUTIFUL BABY IN THE MIDDLE OF THAT BATTLE.
YES--BUT WE--
THE AFFECTION AND PASSION FOR THIS LANTERN WAS IN YOUR EYES EVEN THEN.
SAPPHIRE, PLEASE, HE'S--
YOUR HEART...
...IS HIS HEART.
...HIS HEART IS YOUR HEART...

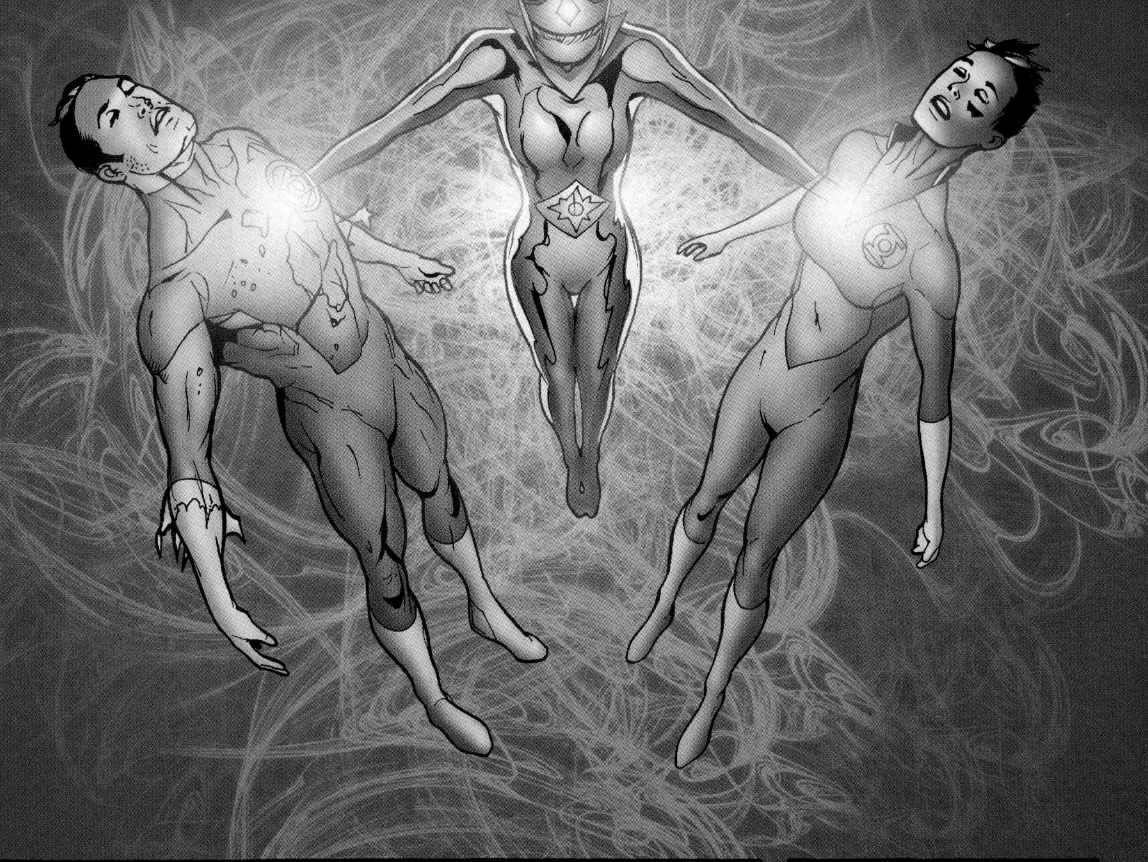
...AND WITH AN INFUSION OF LOVE AND WILL...
...TWO HEARTS ARE ONE!

AAGGHH!

NATU...
KYLE-- I DON'T BELIEVE IT-- YOU'RE BACK...
...YOU CAME BACK TO ME...
I DIDN'T WANT TO KEEP YOU WAITING.
KYLE RAYNER OF THE PLANET EARTH.
AND I'M SURE I HAVE YOU TO THANK, TOO, FOR BEING DOWN AMONG THE LIVING AGAIN.
YOU HAVE ONLY YOUR LOVE TO THANK.
BUT FIRST THINGS FIRST...
YOU HAVE THE ABILITY TO OVERCOME GREAT FEAR.

WELCOME TO THE
GREEN LANTERN CORPS
FEELS LIKE I NEVER LEFT.
WHAT'S THE SITUATION?

YOU BLEW AWAY HUNDREDS OF THEM, KYLE, AND THEIR DARK CONSTRUCT TOO.
BUT THE REMAINING BLACK LANTERNS ARE STILL FOCUSED ON DEVOURING THE BATTERY AND...
AND WHAT?
GUY.

YEAH, GUY WHAT?
SEEING YOU DIE--IT PUSHED HIM OVER THE EDGE, KYLE--VICE'S RING FOUND HIM--FED OFF HIS RAGE.

"GUY'S A RED LANTERN."

NOT FOR LONG HE'S NOT...

...BECAUSE WE'RE JUST GOING TO HAVE TO GET THAT RING OFF MY BUDDY'S HAND RIGHT --

--NOW.
HNN.
WE MAY HAVE A LITTLE MORE FIREPOWER ON OUR SIDE THAN WE THOUGHT.

"I GUESS MOGO DOES SOCIALIZE AFTER ALL."

GREEN LANTERN CORPS 44
over by Patrick Gleason and
ebecca Buchman with Randy Mayor

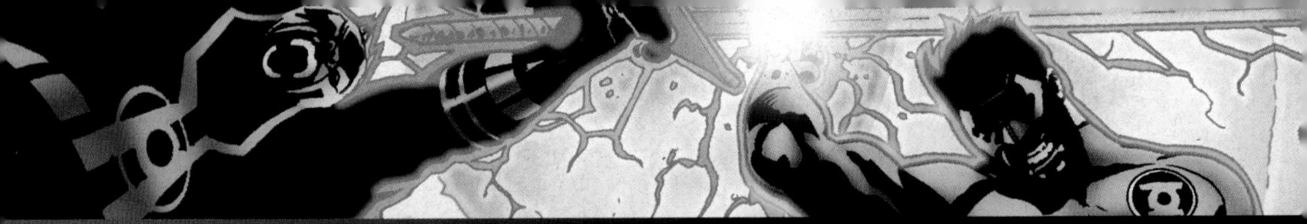

RED BADGE OF RAGE
PART TWO

PATRICK GLEASON
PENCILS

REBECCA BUCHMAN
TOM NGUYEN
KEITH CHAMPAGNE
PATRICK GLEASON
INKS

SECTOR 8.

"MOGO'S SHOWING NO MOVEMENT WHATSOEVER."

WHAT'S HE DOING HERE, SALAAK?
IT'S A PLANET, RAYNER.
OKAY, WHAT'S IT DOING?
THE CITADEL.
IT SEEMS TO BE WAITING.
WAITING FOR WHAT?
I HAVE NO IDEA.

MOGO IS HERE OF ITS OWN VOLITION.
IT MUST HAVE RECEIVED THE DISTRESS CALL FOR ALL LANTERNS TO REPORT TO OA SO--

SO MOGO'S REPORTING FOR DUTY?
OBVIOUSLY.

WELL, UNTIL MOGO DECIDES ON A COURSE OF ACTION TO TAKE, WE NEED TO--
WHAT KIND OF ACTION COULD MOGO POSSIBLY TAKE?
YOU MEAN ASIDE FROM SLAMMING INTO OA AND DECIMATING EVERYONE?
YEAH, ASIDE FROM THAT.
I HAVE NO IDEA.
MIGHT I SUGGEST WE CONCENTRATE ON THE MATTERS AT HAND THAT WE CAN DO SOMETHING ABOUT...
...SUCH AS THESE REMAINING BLACK LANTERNS DEVOURING YOUR CENTRAL BATTERY...

"...AND YOUR FELLOW LANTERN WITH THE *RED RING* ON HIS HAND."

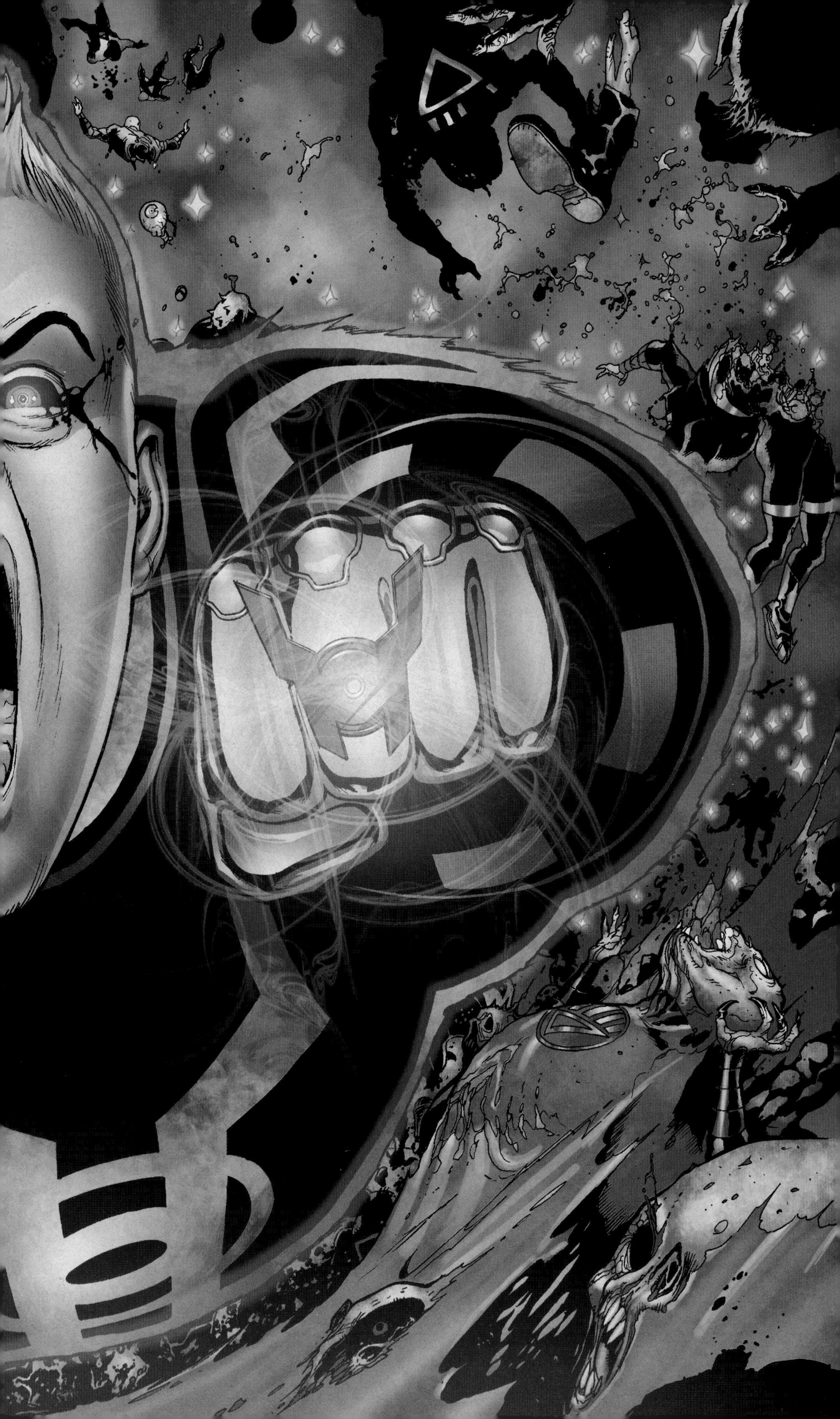

PARTS OF THE BATTERY ARE GOING BLACK!
IT'S NO USE!
THERE'RE TOO MANY OF THEM!
DEVOUR WILL.
DEVOUR WILL.
RAAAGH!
KILL THE DEAD!
KILL 'EM AGAIN!
SHUNK
AND AGAIN!
THEY WANT BLACK?!?
GIVE 'EM BLACK!
THE BLAC
OF FREAKIN
OBLIVION!

SORA, I'M GOING AFTER GUY--YOU AND THE OTHERS WIPE THESE DAMN GREASE MARKS OFF OUR BATTERY BEFORE THERE'S NO BATTERY LEFT TO--
CONNECTION SEVERED.
CONNECTION SEVERED.
NO!
THE BATTERY'S FALLING!
WARNING: CENTRAL POWER BATTERY FOUNDATION DESTABILIZED.
DEVOUR WILL.
DEVOUR WILL.
RING ENERGY ON MY VECTOR!
THE BLACK ENERGY'S DISSIPATING OUR CONSTRUCT!
IT'S NOT HOLDING!

HHOOOO

FFFFFWWWWWROOOOOOOOOOOOOOOOOOOOOOOOOOOOSSSSHHHHHHHH
PLANETWIDE EMERGENCY.
DEBRIS FIELD SPEED TWO HUNDRED MILES AN HOUR.
ENERGY SPHERES RECOMMENDED.
THE DUST CLOUD'S DISSIPATING, WE SHOULD BE ABLE TO HEAD OUT IN A FEW SECONDS TO--
WAIT... THERE'S SOMEONE OUT THERE ALL THIS...
...OMIGOD...
GUY.

ILL! KILL! KILL!
DEVOUR WILL.
DEVOUR WILL.
GUY!
RAYNER-- NO--WAIT!
GET THE HELL OFF!
THAT RED RING'S ON HIS FINGER BECAUSE OF ME!
IF ANYONE CAN GET THROUGH GUY'S RAGE, I CAN!
ONCE HE SEES I'M ALIVE HE'LL--
STOP DOING WHAT HE'S DOING, AND WE CAN'T AFFORD THAT RIGHT NOW!

WHAT THE HELL ARE YOU TALKING ABOUT, VATH?!?
WITH THE RED AND GREEN RINGS ON, GARDNER'S COMPLETELY DESTROYING THESE BLACK LANTERNS--HIS BODY COUNT'S TRIPLE TO THE AMOUNT WE CAN PUT DOWN WITH MUNK!
YOU'RE TELLING ME TO LET GUY STAY A RED LANTERN SO THAT--
I'M SAYING LET'S GIVE GARDNER A WIDE BERTH FOR AS LONG AS POSSIBLE AND LET HIM DO WHAT YOU ORIGINALLY WANTED VICE TO DO.
WE CAN FOCUS ON THE OTHER SIDE OF THE CENTRAL BATTERY WITH MUNK AND TRY TO--
NO!
UNACCEPTABLE!
WE DON'T KNOW WHAT KIND OF DAMAGE THAT RED RING IS CAUSING GUY.
YAARGHH!
C'MON!
HRRN--
...K-KY--

GUY.
IT'S ME... KYLE.
RRRGH-- S-SAW YOU DIE...
THE STAR SAPPHIRE AND SORANIK BROUGHT ME BACK SOMEHOW--I GOT MY--
RRNN--GREEN RING IS BACK--
YEAH, BUT WE HAVE TO GET THAT RED RING OFF YOU AND LET YOUR GREEN RING--
GRRAH-- NO--I LIKE IT-- I LIKE SEEING RED--
--IT'S SIMPLE-- NO MORE GRAY--NO MORE BLACK AND WHITE--NO MORE GREEN--JUST RED--
--RED IS ALL THERE IS!
ZZZRAK
AGGH!
WE DON'T HAVE MUCH TIME, GUY! OUR BATTERY'S BEING EATEN AWAY BY THESE DAMN THINGS--WE HAVE TO STOP THEM!!
UFF!
SKLANG

GUY! LISTEN TO ME, DAMN IT!
I'M NOT DEAD--YOU DON'T NEED TO LET THIS RED RING CONTROL YOU ANYMORE!
LET IT GO--LET ALL THE ANGER AND HATE GO!
YOU'RE A GREEN LANTERN--THIS IS NOT YOU!
RGRGH!

K-KYLE...
YEAH, BUDDY--THAT'S RIGHT IT'S ME--PLEASE DON'T LET IT WIN...WE CAN FIX THIS...
KYLE...DOIN' BEST I...CAN TO KEEP IT FROM SPILLIN' OVER...RED RING'S...TAKING ME WHERE I DON'T WANNA GO...DON'T LET IT...YA GOTTA K-KILL ME BEFORE I...

NO WAY, GUY--THERE'S STILL TIME TO--
RRAGHH--TIME'S UP!
YOU'RE NOT YOU!
BLACK LANTERN TRICK--NOT GIVING INTO IT--
YOU'RE DEAD!
KYLE RAYNER'S DEAD!

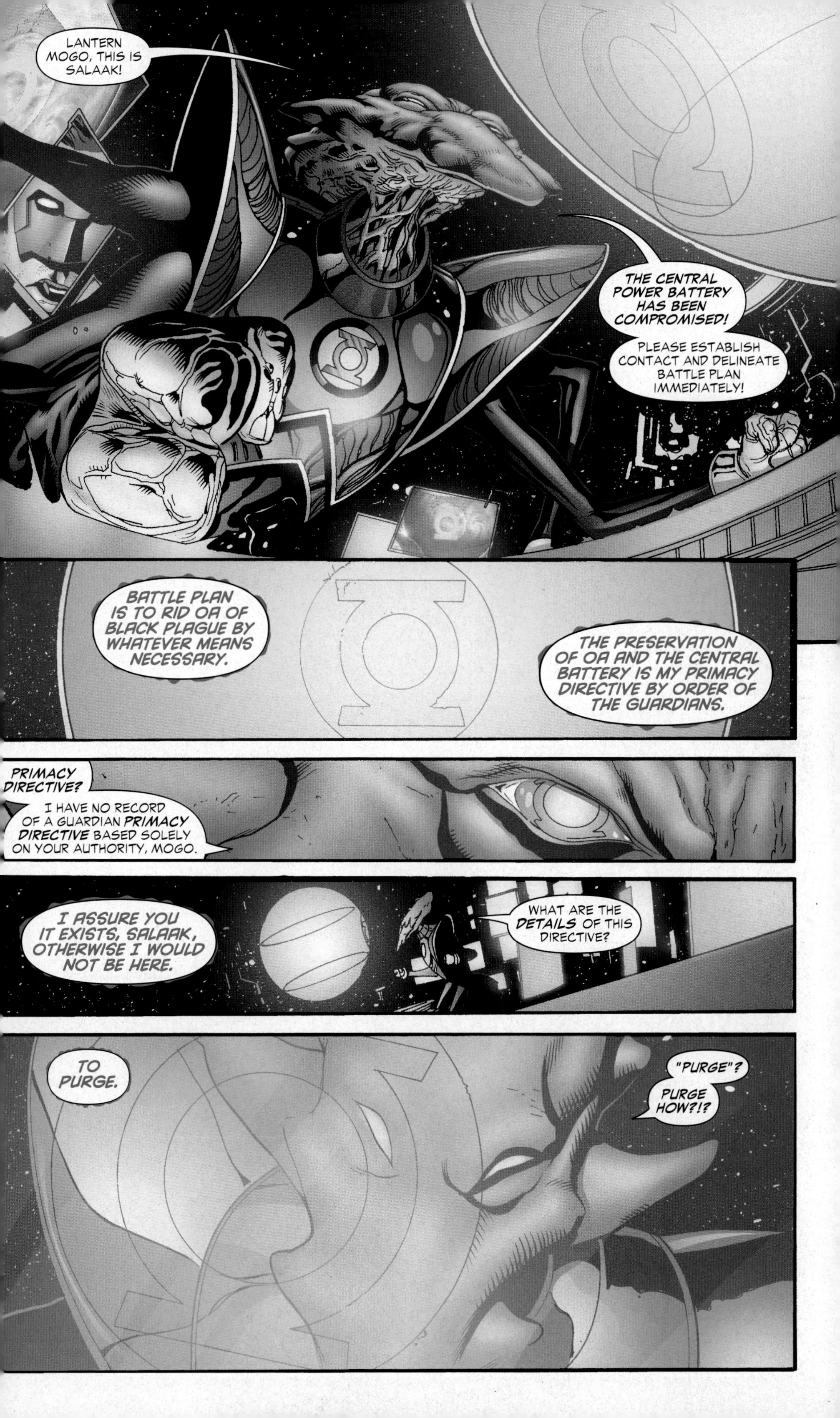
LANTERN MOGO, THIS IS SALAAK!
THE CENTRAL POWER BATTERY HAS BEEN COMPROMISED!
PLEASE ESTABLISH CONTACT AND DELINEATE BATTLE PLAN IMMEDIATELY!
BATTLE PLAN IS TO RID OA OF BLACK PLAGUE BY WHATEVER MEANS NECESSARY.
THE PRESERVATION OF OA AND THE CENTRAL BATTERY IS MY PRIMACY DIRECTIVE BY ORDER OF THE GUARDIANS.
PRIMACY DIRECTIVE?
I HAVE NO RECORD OF A GUARDIAN PRIMACY DIRECTIVE BASED SOLELY ON YOUR AUTHORITY, MOGO.
I ASSURE YOU IT EXISTS, SALAAK, OTHERWISE I WOULD NOT BE HERE.
WHAT ARE THE DETAILS OF THIS DIRECTIVE?
TO PURGE.
"PURGE"?
PURGE HOW?!?

RAAAGH!
SALAAK! WHAT THE HELL'S MOGO DOING?!?
SKKRRRKKKK
MOGO USED THE TERM PURGE!
PURGE WHAT-- US?!?
I AM AFRAID MOGO DID NOT ELABORATE.
THE PLANET IS SUCKING US INTO SPACE!
HE'S NOT JUS SUCKING US UP, SWEETIE.
YOUR FEEDING TIME IS OVER, VILE ONES.

RING'S NOT WORKING!
I CAN'T GENERATE A CONSTRUCT!
ME EITHER-- BUT OUR ENERGY AURA'S BEEN ACTIVATED!

YOU WILL DEFILE OUR BATTERY NO MORE.
...HE'S SUCKING UP EVERYONE...

OA WILL BE CLEANSED OF YOUR TOXIC PRESENCE.
...GOOD GUYS AND BA GUYS!

ATTENTION ALL LANTERNS.
DUE TO THE INFESTATION OF BLACK LANTERNS ON OA I HAVE INCREASED MY GRAVITATIONAL PULL EXPONENTIALLY.
AS A RESULT ALL ORGANIC MATERIAL IS BEING DRAWN TO MY SURFACE FOR CONSUMPTION.
I APOLOGIZE FOR THE INCONVENIENCE.
CHOMP
IMMINENT IMPACT IN FOUR MINUTES.
DUE TO INTERRUPTION OF YOUR POWER RINGS AND PROXIMITY OF BLACK LANTERNS, HAND-TO-HAND COMBAT IS RECOMMENDED.
IMPACT IN THREE MINUTES.
IMPACT IN TWO MINUTES.
IMPACT IN ONE MINUTE.

THE SURFACE OF MOGO.
IT'S BEGUN?
YES, IOLANDE.
THERE IS NO NEED TO FEAR FOR THE SAFETY OF THE WOUNDED LANTERNS YOU ESCORTED HERE.
SHOULD I--

WHAT THE--
WE'VE STOPPED FALLING!
BUT THE BLACK LANTERN HAVEN'T!
IMPACT IN FIVE SECONDS.

THEY CONTINUE TO BE UNDER MY PROTECTION AND CARE UNTIL THEY ARE COMPLETELY HEALED.
THE PARASITES THAT WREAKED HAVOC ON OA WILL BE NEUTRALIZED AT AN ISOLATED LOCATION.

THAT FIELD OF GRASS...

...MOGO'S PULLING THEM UNDER.

THEY'RE DROWNING...

PURGE OF OA COMPLETE.
...IN A SEA OF GREEN.

ALL THE BLACK LANTERNS WILL BE PULLED THROUGH EACH STRATUM OF MY BEING.
THEY WILL BE TORN ASUNDER AND DIFFUSED.
SIFTED INTO ATOMS.
UNTIL ALL THAT IS LEFT OF THEM...
...WILL BE DRAWN TO THE CENTER OF MY CORE...
...WHERE THEY WILL FOREVER BE SUPERHEATED AND PREVENTED FROM RE-FORMING.
IN OTHER WORDS, MY FELLOW LANTERNS...
...THEY WILL BURN FOR ALL ETERNITY.

I'VE ORDERED ALL THE LANTERNS BACK TO OA AS SALAAK REQUESTED.
GOOD, BECAUSE SINCE MOGO'S GOT THE BLACK LANTERNS UNDER HIS THUMB...
...OUR ONLY PRIORITY IS TO FIND GUY AND GET THAT DAMN RED RING OFF AS SOON AS--
DON'T WORRY...
...I'VE FOUND YOU.

GREEN LANTERN CORPS 45
Cover by Patrick Gleason and Rebecca Buchman with Randy Mayor

RED DAWN

PATRICK GLEASON
PENCILS

REBECCA BUCHMAN
KEITH CHAMPAGNE
TOM NGUYEN
INKS

RRRRR
RED IS GREEN.
GREEN IS RED.
DON'T RAISE YOUR RINGS.
WE'RE NOT FIGHTING BACK--WE'RE NOT FEEDING HIS RAGE.
I LOOK AT YOUR FACES AND I SEE FRIENDS-- PEOPLE I CARE ABOUT--AND I KNOW--
--THAT YOU'RE MY ENEMIES--
--THAT YOU NEED TO BE RIPPED APART AND BURNED UNTIL THERE'S NOTHING LEFT!
I'M NOT GONNA JUST STAND HERE AND LET HIM--
ANY SHOW OF FORCE WILL PUSH HIM OVER THE EDGE, VATH. WE HAVE TO--
LOOK AT HIS EYES, RAYNER-- HE'S ALREADY FALLEN OVER THAT EDGE.
HE'S PAST SAVING NOW.
I'M GUY GARDNER--I'M A GREEN LANTERN--I PROTECT AND SERVE INNOC--
NO.
GUY GARDNER--I'M A RED LANTERN!
AND I GOT ONE PURPOSE AND ONE PURPOSE ONLY...

...AND THAT'S TO DESTROY EVERYONE AND EVERYTHING THAT STANDS IN MY FREAKIN' WAY!

AAAGH!
YOU'RE JUST GREEN BUGS THAT WANNA KILL ME!
AND I'LL SHOW YA WHAT I DO TO BUGS!
I CRUSH 'EM!
FZZRAKK
VATH'S RIGHT! GUY'S TOO FAR GONE--
SHIELDS UP--FIRE FOR EFFECT!
NNNH!
RED IS PURE!
RED IS RIGHT!
GO AHEAD--THROW YOUR COLORS AT ME!
RED WILL BURN THEM ALL!
STILL IN A COMPASSIONATE MOOD THERE, MUNK?!?
ALWAYS.
BUT COMPASSION MUST SOMETIMES BE TEMPERED WITH MIGHT.

WATCH OUT--HE IS AARGH!
SCREAM! SCREAM TO ME!
I'M GOING TO TRY TO RECONNECT HIM WITH HIS HUMANITY--
UNNN!
--OPEN HIS HEART WITH A SAPPHIRE TETHER.
SHUNK
RRRARGHH!
RRRRRRR

SAPPHIRE!
YAAAA!
I CAN'T HOLD HIM--
--HE'S TOO STRONG!
TOGETHER!
ANCHOR HIM!
ONLY ONE WAY--
RRRGHH!
IT'S NOT WORKING!
HE'S STARTING TO URN THROUGH MY ENERGY TETHER!
MOGO!
GUY'S DRAGGING US AROUND LIKE CANS BEHIND A WEDDING CAR!

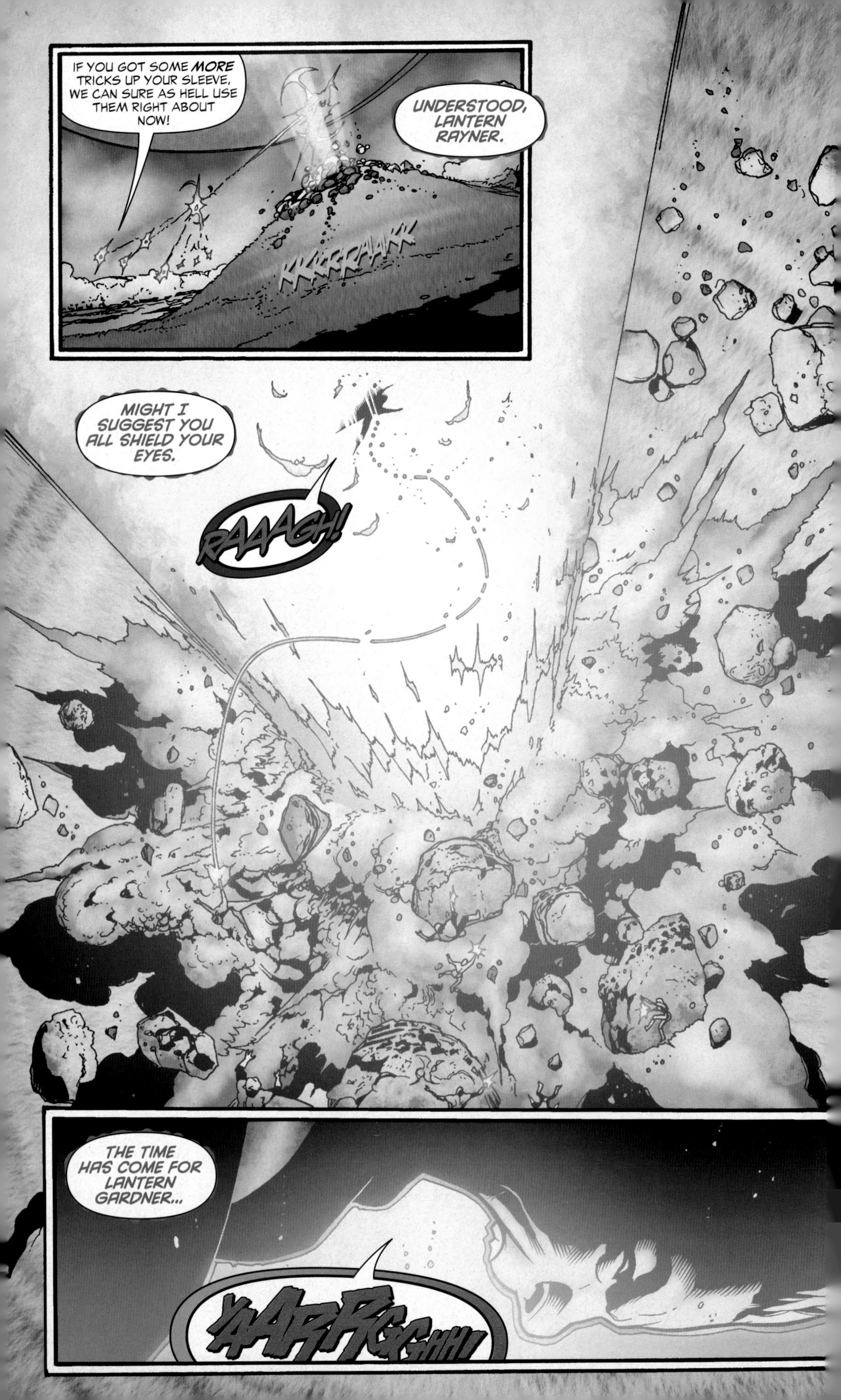
IF YOU GOT SOME MORE TRICKS UP YOUR SLEEVE, WE CAN SURE AS HELL USE THEM RIGHT ABOUT NOW!
UNDERSTOOD, LANTERN RAYNER.
KKKRRAAKK
MIGHT I SUGGEST YOU ALL SHIELD YOUR EYES.
RAAAGH!
THE TIME HAS COME FOR LANTERN GARDNER...
YAARRGGHHH

...TO SEE HIS
FE THROUGH THE
ED AND GREEN OF
THE RINGS...
NNAARGHH!
...AND THE DISTINCT WAY THAT ALL HE HAS KNOWN AND EXPERIENCED MAKES HIM THE BEING HE IS TODAY.
THE GOOD.
UNNNN!
POOM
THE BAD.
HOLY--
MOGO-- WHAT THE HELL--
THE UGLY.
...NO...

CLASS OF

NOOOOOOO

BACK!
STAY BACK!
...TORA...
I'M WAITING FOR YOU, GUY.
WHEN ARE YOU COMING BACK--
--TO ME?
WHAT MAKES YOU THINK YOU DESERVE HER, BOY?!?
WHAT MAKES YOU THINK YOU DESERVE A LOVE LIKE THIS?

ONLY THING YOU'VE EVER BEEN GOOD AT IS NEVER COMING IN FIRST!
AND THE ONLY THING YOU WERE EVER GOOD AT, DAD, WAS BEING A BASTARD!
GUY'S STRUGGLING AGAINST BOTH SIDES OF HIMSELF!
WE'VE GOT TO HELP BLAST THE RED CONSTRUCTS!
FZZRAKK
NO.
FZZRAKK
LANTERN GARDNER NEEDS TO BATTLE THESE PERSONAL DEMONS ALONE.
THERE'S NO WINNER'S CIRCLE WAITING FOR YOU LIKE THERE WAS FOR YOUR BROTHER MACE!
AND THERE SURE AS HELL AIN'T NO POT O' GOLD AT THE END OF YOUR RAINBOW!
YOU'RE A BRONZE BOY, GUY--
--ALWAYS HAVE BEEN--
--ALWAYS WILL BE!

WE'RE THE GREEN LANTERN CORPS, MOGO!
WE FACE EVERYTHING TOGETHER--
--EVEN OUR DAMN DEMONS!
C'MON, LET'S SWING THIS THING AND MASH THOSE CONSTRUCTS!
YOU'LL FIND OUT NO ONE CARES ABOUT PEOPLE AT THE BOTTOM OF THE BARREL, GUY!
ESPECIALLY A LOSER LIKE YOU!
BURN--
BURN YOU LIKE THE CANCER YOU WERE ON OUR LIVES!
IT'S HAMMERIN' TIME, POOZERS!

BEFORE GUY CAN FOCUS!
HIM UP TIGHT!
RAAAGH!
COVERED--
SUPPRESS THEIR POWER!
RRMMMFF--
LET'S TRY AND GET THIS RED RING OFF HIM AND LOCKED UP DOWN ON OA.
THAT IS NOT TO BE, LANTERN.
HE RED RING IS NLIKE OUR RINGS. IT DOES NOT IMPLY SLIP OFF AND ON.
ONCE IT FINDS A HOST, IT DOES NOT RELINQUISH ITS GRIP.
THEY ARE BONDED UNTIL...
THE HOST IS DEAD.

SALVATION FROM THE RAGE OF A RED LANTERN.
I'M ALL EARS.
LANTERN CAN CLEANSE A CORRUPTED SOUL AND OBLITERATE A RED RING.
RRRMFMM!
WELL, OKAY THEN, THAT'S WHERE I'M TAKING GUY!
LOCK ON ONE OF THESE BLUE LANTERNS AND BEAM US THERE!
UNFORTUNATELY, I DO NOT HAVE ENOUGH POWER TO TRANSPORT ANYONE AT THIS TIME.
SHUNK SHUNK SHUNK
THEN GIVE ME THE COORDINATES OF ONE OF THESE BLUE LANTERNS AND WE'LL TAKE HIM THERE OURSELVES.
WITH ALL OUR RINGS WE'LL KEEP GUY RESTRAINED AND--
I AM AFRAID THAT WILL NOT BE POSSIBLE.
"WILL NOT"--"DO NOT"--"DOES NOT"-- YOU'RE NOT SAYING ANYTHING I WANT TO HEAR RIGHT NOW--
--SO LET ME WORRY ABOUT WHAT'S POSSIBLE!
GIVE ME THE DAMN LOCATION OF THE--
KYLE...
NO!
ENOUGH'S ENOUGH!
HOW MANY PEOPLE THAT I CARE ABOUT DO I NEED TO LOS BEFORE ENOUGH IS ENOUGH?!?
HOW MANY?!
RRMMM!

YOU WOULD
T BE ABLE TO
O VERY FAR,
LANTERN.
THE RED LANTERN'S
POWER IS GROWING
NSIDE HIM EVEN AS WE
PEAK. THE RESTRAINTS
WILL ONLY HOLD HIM
FOR SO LONG.
WE WERE ABLE TO KEEP RED LANTERN VICE LOCKED UP IN A SCIENCELL, SO I'VE GOT NO DOUBT THAT--
RAAAGH!
THESE "SCIENCELLS"-- DID THEY HAPPEN TO BE CREATED BY THE GUARDIANS FOR EACH SPECIFIC PRISONER'S PARTICULAR DISPOSITION?
...YEAH...
THEN *THAT* IS WHY YOU WERE ABLE TO CONTAIN THE RED LANTERN KNOWN AS VICE DOWN BELOW ON OA.
WE'RE KINDA ALL OUT OF GUARDIANS AT THE MOMENT, MUNK, SO THERE SURE AS HELL AREN'T MANY OPTIONS HERE!
BUT I'LL TELL YOU ONE OF THOSE OPTIONS IS *NOT* LEAVING MY FRIEND LIKE *THIS!*
RAARGH!
SORA, THERE HAS TO BE SOMETHING WE CAN DO?
RING.
FULL BODY-SCAN OF GUY GARDNER.
RED RING INFESTATION DETECTED THROUGHOUT.
LANTERN GARDNER'S HEART AND BLOOD SUPPLY HAS BEEN COMPLETELY COMPROMISED.

GUY'S GONNA BE BREAKING THROUGH THOSE THINGS SOON.
HE'S MOVED ON FROM KILLING BLACK LANTERNS TO TRYING TO KILL GREEN LANTERNS.
...I KNOW...
RRGHHM!
GRRAGH!
KYLE, WHEN YOU HAD GUY DOWN FOR A FEW SECONDS--YOU WERE TALKING--HE WAS TALKING--WHAT DID HE SAY?
HE SAID GET THE RING OFF HIM--HE SAID "DON'T GIVE UP ON ME, KYLE, WHATEVER YOU DO, DON'T GIVE UP ON ME."
KYLE.
ALRIGHT, HE SAID "YOU GOTTA KILL ME."
OF COURSE HE DID.
WE BOTH KNOW THE LAST THING IN THE WORLD GUY WOULD WANT TO DO IS INJURE OR KILL ANOTHER LANTERN, BUT--
DON'T EVEN THINK IT, KILOWOG.
I DON'T WANT TO, KYLE, BUT THERE'S NO--
DON'T EVEN SAY IT OUT LOUD.
WHAT THE--
MOGO'S PULLED GUY BACK DOWN TO THE SURFACE!
FOOOM

I WILL BEAR LANTERN GARDNER'S RAGE.
RRGAAA!
WHAT ARE YOU TALKING ABOUT, MOGO, HOW WILL--
TRUST ME, LANTERN RAYNER.
I AM NOW IMMERSING GUY IN A NUTRIENT BATH TO KEEP HIS BODY FROM GOING INTO SHOCK.
RRMMMF!
SHOCK? WHY WOULD HIS BODY GO INTO SHOCK?
BECAUSE HIS ENTIRE BLOOD SUPPLY--
--IS ABOUT TO BE FILTERED AT SUPER-SPEED.

LANTERN GARDNER'S BLOOD WILL BECOME MY BLOOD.
NAARGRHH!
UGH, THOSE LEACHES ARE BURROWING RIGHT THROUGH HIS DAMN SKIN AND DOWN HIS THROAT.
YES. THEY'RE COURSING THROUGH HIS ENTIRE BODY.
AMAZING. THEY'RE LIKE SUPER-ANTIBODIES...
...ATTACKING NOT ONLY CORRUPTED VITAL ORGANS, BUT EACH AND EVERY CELL IN HIS BODY.
GARDNER'S RAGE-FILLED HEART AND BODY WILL BE CLEANSED, MY FELLOW LANTERNS.

SON OF A BITCH.

GUY.
...H-HEY...

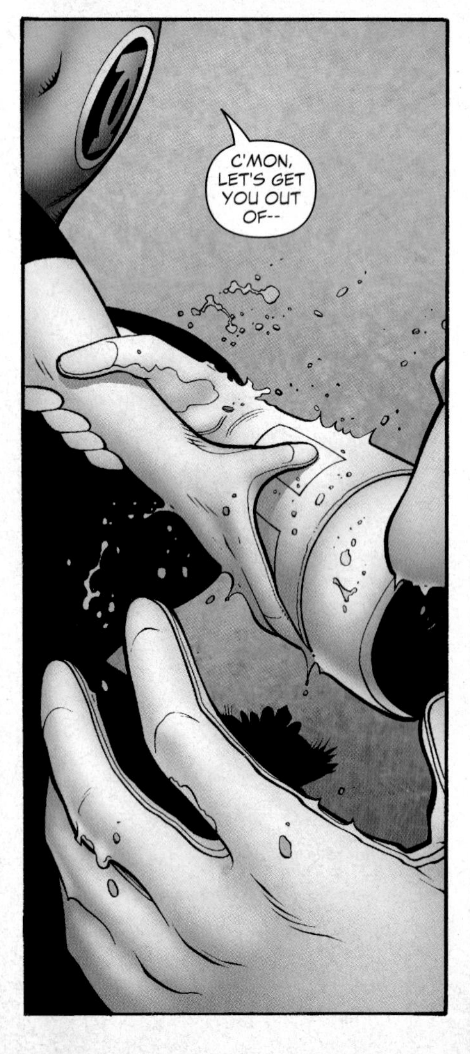
C'MON, LET'S GET YOU OUT OF--

--THERE.

THOUGHT I LOST YA TO THAT BLACK RING, BUDDY.
THOUGHT WE LOST YOU TOO.
IT'S LIKE WAKING FROM A FREAKIN' NIGHTMARE.
AND YOU DIDN'T GIVE UP ON ME.
NONE OF YOU.
PLEASE TELL ME I DIDN'T KILL ANY--
ONLY THE BAD GUYS, POOZER, ONLY THE BAD GUYS.
JUST ROUGHED UP SOME OF US LANTERNS A BIT-- NOTHING TOO SERIOUS.
SHEESH, THAT'S A FREAKIN' RELIEF.
JUST HOW THE HELL DID YOU GET THE RED RING OFF MY HAND?
YOU DON'T REMEMBER?
IT'S ALL JUST ONE RED BLUR.
MOGO GOT IT OFF-- MOGO SAVED YOU.
IF I COULD GET MY ARMS AROUND YA, I'D GIVE YA A BIG HUG, YA BIG LUG!
NO NEED TO THANK ME, LANTERN GARDNER. WE ARE ALL PART OF THE SAME TEAM.
BUT BEFORE YOU DEPART, HEED THIS WARNING.

I HAVE DONE ALL THAT I CAN, YET THERE ARE STILL TRACE AMOUNTS OF TOXIC RED LANTERN BLOOD COURSING THROUGH YOUR SYSTEM.
AS THE INDIGO LANTERN STATED, ONLY THE LIGHT OF A BLUE LANTERN CAN COMPLETELY ERADICATE THE EXPOSURE TO A RED RING.
GOT IT. RED BAD, BLUE GOOD.

OKAY, I KNOW WHO SAVED MY ASS, KYLE, BUT WHO SAVED YOURS?
MIRI. THE STAR SAPPHIRE.

GOOD GOING, KID. YOU GOT YOURSELF AN OPEN TAB AT WARRIORS BAR FER LIFE.
I APPRECIATE THE GESTURE BUT--
FOOD AND BOOZE MIND YA, NOT JUST--
UNNN.

WHAT IS IT, MUNK?
I SENSE REVERBERATIONS IN THE TIME/SPACE CONTINUUM--MEMBERS OF THE INDIGO TRIBE ARE AT THIS MOMENT LOCKING IN ON YOUR CENTRAL POWER BATTERY.
WE NEED TO RETURN TO OA IMMEDIATELY.

THEN LET'S STOP BURNING DAYLIGHT AND GO ROLL OUT THE GREEN CARPET...

...AND SEE WHAT THE HELL THEY WANT.
...SO CONSIDER YOURSELVES NOW UPDATED, THERE IS NO TIME TO WASTE.
FAASSH
MANY OF OUR BRETHREN, EVEN AS WE SPEAK, ARE GATHERING LANTERNS FROM ALL THE CORPS WORLDS ACROSS THE UNIVERSE.
THAT IS WHY WE ARE HERE TO TRANSPORT YOU.
AND THAT IS WHY WE MUST LEAVE NOW IF WE HOLD ANY HOPE OF DEFEATING NEKRON.
NOT ONLY WITH YOU, BUT WITH AS MANY OF YOUR FELLOW CORPS MEMBERS AS POSSIBLE.
THE BATTLEFIELD IS THE THIRD PLANET FROM SOL--EARTH.
NOBODY SCREWS WITH MY HOMETOWN!
OUR HOMETOWN!
ALL LANTERNS POWER UP!
RECHARGE!

IN BRIGHTEST DAY, IN BLACKEST NIGHT, NO EVIL SHALL ESCAPE OUR SIGHT.
LET THOSE WHO WORSHIP EVIL'S MIGHT
BEWARE OUR POWER--GREEN LANTERNS
LIGHT.

GREEN LANTERN CORPS 46
Cover by Patrick Gleason and
Rebecca Buchman with Randy Mayor

BLACK DAWN

PATRICK GLEASON
PENCILS

REBECCA BUCHMAN
KEITH CHAMPAGNE
TOM NGUYEN
INKS

EARTH'S ORBIT.
GOT US A
EGULAR RING
F FIRE GOING
HERE!
AAAIIEEEE!
NOW THIS IS AN ALLIANCE FOR THE BOOK OF OA!
A CHAPTER I'M SURE THE GUARDIANS WOULD LIKE TO LEAVE OUT IF THEY EVER GET A CHANCE TO WRITE IT!
CONNECTION SEVERED.
AND I'M SURE THESE RED LANTERNS WOULD HAVE NO PROBLEM BURNING US WITH IT WHEN THEY GET THE CHANCE!
I'D SURE LIKE TO SHAKE THE HAND OF WHOEVER RIPPED ARKILLO'S TONGUE OUT, ARISIA.
WHY'S THAT, KILOWOG?
'CAUSE A LITTLE PEACE AND QUIET IN THE MIDDLE OF A FIREFIGHT GOES A LONG WAY.
KIKK KIKKIKK
YEAH, YEAH, I SEE 'EM! KEEP FIRING, BEDOVIAN!
AAAIIEEEE!
CONNECTION SEVERED.
I ALWAYS HATED CATS--THERE'S SOMETHING ABOUT 'EM I DON'T TRUST!
ESPECIALLY ONES THAT CAN INCINERATE ANYTHING WITHIN A FEW FEET OF THEIR WHISKERS!
SORRY TO INTRUDE ON WHAT SEEMS TO BE AN IMPORTANT CONVERSATION, BUT I DO GET THE SENSE...

...THAT WE ARE DANGEROUSLY CLOSE TO BEING OVERRUN!

"THOLIAN WEB"?
YEAH, STAR TREK, THE ORIGINAL SERIES, SEASON THREE, EPISODE 64.
SOMETIMES YOU REALLY DO SCARE ME, GUY.
OKAY, SINCE WE'RE ALL HOLDING HANDS AND SINGING KUMBAYA, IT'S TIME TO MAKE A SERIOUS DENT IN THE AMOUNT OF THESE BLACK LANTERNS!
I SAY WE GO THOLIAN WEB ON THEIR ASSES!
LOOK, IT'LL WORK, EVERYONE JUST FOLLOW MY FREAKIN' LEAD!
AND WHAT MAKES YOU THINK I'M GOING TO FOLLOW THE PLAN OF A GREEN LANTERN?
HEY, I KNOW I AIN'T GOT A CHANCE AT WINNING A STARING CONTEST WITH YOU...
...BUT DON'T YA WANNA WIPE THESE THINGS OUT SO WE CAN GET BACK TO KILLING EACH OTHER AGAIN?
YES.
GOOD, THEN SHUT YER UGLY YAP, WE GOT WORK TO DO!

AWRIGHT, REDS, ELLOWS, VIOLETS AND NDIGOS--GET READY TO RECEIVE A GENERAL FREQUENCY TRANSMISSION!
I'M UPLOADING THE PLAN TO YOUR RINGS SO THERE'S NO FREAKIN' CONFUSION--SO GET GOING AND LET YOUR RINGS DO THE TALKING!
HATE TO BREAK UP THE PARTY, BUT THIS SITUATION'S GONNA GET WORSE BEFORE IT GETS BETTER.
HOW MUCH WORSE?
XANSHI.
THE PLANET?
YEAH.
THE ONE THAT YOU, UH...
DESTROYED. YES, IT'S NOW A BLACK LANTERN.
THE *WHOLE* FREAKIN' PLANET XANSHI'S A BLACK LANTERN?!
AND *IT'S* HEADING OUR WAY.
BUT NOT IF YOU CAN HELP IT.
DAMN RIGHT, WOG.
THEN LET'S GET A SQUAD TOGETHER...
...BECAUSE I'M GOING WITH YOU.

AWRIGHT, FIRE!
LET'S SCOOP UP THESE BLACK LANTERNS IN OUR *TRAWLING WEB* UNTIL THEY POP THE WEASEL!
CONNECTION SEVERED.
CONNECTION SEVERED.
CONNECTION SEVERED.
CONNECTION SEVERED.
CONNECTION SEVERED.
CONNECTION SEVERED.
CONNECTION SEVERED.
CONNECTION SEVERED.
CONNECTION SEVERED.
CONNECTION SEVERED.
CONNECTION SEVERED.
CONNECTIO SEVERED.
CONNECTION SEVERED.
CONNECTION SEVERED.
CONNECTION SEVERED.

CONNECTION SEVERED.
CONNECTION SEVERED.
CONNECTION SEVERED.
CONNECTION SEVERED.
CONNECTION SEVERED.
CONNECTION SEVERED.

CONNECTION SEVERED.
CONNECTION SEVERED.
CONNECTION SEVERED.
CONNECTION SEVERED.
CONNECTION SEVERED.
CONNECTION SEVERED.
CONNECTION SEVERED.
CONNECTION SEVERED.
PULL!
KEEP THEM CONTAINED!
DON'T LET ANY SLIP THROUGH!
CRAP!
WHAT?
I THINK WE'RE GONNA NEED A BIGGER NET.
HOW MANY?
I DON'T KNOW, GIVE OR TAKE...

...A HUNDRED THOUSAND!
RAPID ENERGY LOSS OF WEB CONSTRUCT.
BRACE FOR IMPACT.
ENERGY WEB DISSIPATING.
FORCEFUL COLLISION IMMINENT.
NAARGHH!
HELLO, GUY...
UNNN--

...I WAS WONDERING WHEN YOU'D *FINALLY* COME BACK HOME TO VISIT.
LOOKS LIKE ALL IT TOOK WAS ANOTHER DISASTER TO GET YOUR ATTENTION...
OMIGOD... *ICE...*
...FOR YOU TO FINALLY REALIZE WHAT'S IMPORTANT--*WHO'S* IMPORTANT IN YOUR LIFE.
TORA-- NO--YOU CAN'T BE DEAD-- PLEASE--
SEEMS YOU'RE A LITTLE LATE AS USUAL, GUY.
WHAT DID THEY DO TO YOU, DAMN IT?!?
THEY DIDN'T DO ANYTHING TO ME. IT'S WHAT *YOU* DID, WHAT YOU'VE *BEEN* DOING TO ME ALL THESE YEARS.
YOU COULDN'T JUST COME AND VISIT ME--SURPRISE ME--SHOW ME THAT I ACTUALLY MEAN SOMETHING TO YOU--THAT I'M NOT JUST A WARM BODY TO KEEP YOU FROM GETTING COLD WHEN YOU'RE BORED AND LONELY!
SO MANY PROMISES...SO MANY WASTED PROMISES.

IS THIS ALL YOU GOT, NEKRON?!? IS THIS ALL YOU HAVE LEFT TO PLAY?!?
THESE "DEATH" CARDS YOU KEEP SHOVING IN OUR FACES?!
I'M DONE PLAYING YOUR GAMES!
I'M NOT OPENING--
ALEX!
COME INSIDE, KYLE.
WE'VE GOT SOOOO MUCH TO TALK ABOUT--

--SO MUCH TO CATCH UP ON!
SHLUMP
YOU MISSED ALL THE FUN THE DAY I DIED.
I THINK IT'S TIME YOU EXPERIENCED IT FIRSTHAND.
NO!
YOU SHOULD'VE SEEN THE LOOK ON MAJOR FORCE'S FACE WHEN HE REALIZED YOU WEREN'T HOME, KYLE.
MAKE THIS STOP!

TORA! THIS BLACK FREAKIN' RING IS--
YOU'RE HERE BECAUSE YOU NEED TO BE HERE, GUY, NOT BECAUSE YOU WANT TO BE HERE.
YOUR JOB--BEING A LANTERN--SIMPLY MEANS MORE TO YOU THAN I DO.
YOU ONLY CONNECT WITH OTHER PEOPLE WHEN IT'S CONVENIENT--WHEN IT FILLS THE HOLE IN YOUR SOUL.
THE TORA I LOVE KNOWS THAT'S NOT TRUE, AND YOU'RE NOT HER!
IF YOU'RE SO SURE ABOUT THAT, GUY, THEN END IT-- END ME!
BEING KILLED AND RESURRECTED AND KILLED AGAIN-- IT'S TOO MUCH...
...I'M SO TIRED--TIRED OF REBUILDING MY LIFE OVER AND OVER-- ONLY TO HAVE IT STOLEN AWAY FROM ME AGAIN AND AGAIN.
COMPASSION.
NO!
I WON'T DO IT!

THEN I GUESS I'LL HAVE TO WAIT A FEW SECONDS UNTIL WE HIT THE GROUND AND SHATTER--
--BECAUSE MAYBE THEN I'LL FINALLY BE ABLE TO REALLY HAVE A PIECE OF YOUR HEART!
THE ONLY ONE GOING TO PIECES TODAY--
--IS WHATEVER BOGUS PIECE OF GARBAGE--
NO-- YOU'RE MINE!
--YOU'VE BE
PRETENDING
BE!

MAJOR FORCE WAS NOT A HAPPY CAMPER--SO HE DECIDED TO TAKE IT OUT ON ME.
FORCE BROKE ALMOST EVERY BONE IN MY BODY AS HE THREW ME AROUND THE APARTMENT--
--AND I FELT EACH AND EVERY ONE SNAP UNTIL HE GOT TO MY SPINE--
KRAKK
--WHICH THANKFULLY SAVED ME FROM FEELING HIS HANDS AROUND MY NECK WHEN HE BROKE THAT TOO...
...AND DECIDED TO HAVE A LITTLE SURPRISE WAITING FOR YOU WHEN YOU GOT HUNGRY.

RRRN!
S-STOP IT...WHAT ARE YOU DOING...
YOU SEE, KYLE, EVERYTHING YOU DID LED MAJOR FORCE TO KILLING ME THAT DAY.
IT WAS AS IF YOU DID IT YOURSELF.
YOUR NOT BEING THERE WAS REALLY JUST A TECHNICALITY.
THERE'S ONLY ONE WAY YOU CAN MAKE SURE IT DOESN'T HAPPEN AGAIN TO SOMEONE ELSE, KYLE.
SO GO AHEAD, PUT THAT ALL-POWERFUL RING UNDER YOUR CHIN AND MAKE IT ALL GO AWAY.
YOU TASTED WHAT I WANT FOR YOU.
A BLACK RING FOUND YOUR FINGER FOR A FEW FLEETING MOMENTS.
YOU NOW UNDERSTAND THE BEAUTY AND SOLITUDE OF NOTHINGNESS.
...SOMETHING'S ALWAYS BETTER...THAN NOTHING...
...AND I KNOW YOUR SPIRIT'S OUT THERE, ALEX, AND I'M SORRY FOR WHAT YOU WENT THROUGH...
...THE PAIN AND SUFFERING ALL BECAUSE YOU CARED ABOUT ME...
ZZRAPPP
ZZRAPPP
IT'S SOMETHING I CAN NEVER MAKE RIGHT NO MATTER HOW MUCH I TRY.
BUT YOU'LL ALWAYS BE IN MY HEART...

...BECAUSE YOUR LOVE HELPED MAKE ME A BETTER MAN, ALEX.
ZZRAPPP
AND I'LL HONOR THAT FOR AS LONG AS I LIVE.
BUT YOU ON THE OTHER HAND...
RRAGH!
...I WON'T!

COME ON, MUNK, I NEED YOUR HELP.
I PRESUME THIS IS SOMEONE YOU ONCE CARED DEEPLY FOR?
YES.
ARE THERE ANY LAST WORDS YOU'D LIKE TO SAY?
YES.
REST IN PEACE, ALEX.
AAAAIIEEEE!
CONNECTION SEVERED.
KYLE! YOU THERE?!?
I'M HERE!
JUST FELL INTO A SITUATION IN COAST CITY THAT'S GONNA NEED SOME SERIOUS RING-SLINGING!
YA KNOW HOW WE'VE NEVER BEEN ABLE TO FIND THE ANTI-MONITOR AFTER SUPER-PUNK TOSSED HIM?
YEAH!

YAARRRGH!!
...BECAUSE I FINALLY FOUND WHERE THAT UGLY BASTARD'S BEEN HIDING!
ON OUR WAY, GUY!
LANTERN RAYNER, I WOULD LIKE TO KNOW MORE ABOUT THIS ANTI-MONITOR BEFORE WE ENGAGE.
THE 411 ON HIM, MIRI, IS AT THE SAME MOMENT OUR UNIVERSE WAS BORN, AN ANTIMATTER UNIVERSE WAS ALSO CREATED. BILLIONS OF YEARS LATER THE ANTI-MONITOR SLOWLY BEGAN TAKING POWER.
HE CONQUERED THE WEAPONERS OF QWARD AND LEARNED FROM THEM THAT THERE WAS A DIFFERENT UNIVERSE, A POSITIVE MATTER UNIVERSE--OURS--AND HE'S WANTED CONTROL OF IT EVER SINCE.

WE'VE PUT THE ANTI-MONITOR DOWN BEFORE, AND WE'LL PUT HIM DOWN AGAIN!
CONNECTION SEVERED.
CONNECTION SEVERED.
CONNECTION SEVERED.
RING, WHY THE HELL'S THE ANTI-MONITOR INSIDE THE BLACK BATTERY.
ALL DATA BEING DISSEMINATED SHOWS THE ANTI-MONITOR IS BEING IMPRISONED BY NEKRON AND UTILIZED AS A MASSIVE ENERGY CELL TO FACILITATE HIS STRATEGY.
SO NEKRON'S DRAINING HIS ASS AND IT'S KILLING HIM?!?
AFFIRMATIVE.
LET ME OUT.

ANTI-MONITOR FROM EVERY POSSIBLE ANGLE!
THAT'S A HALF-FORMED BLACK LANTERN SYMBOL ON HIS CHEST--
--WHICH MEANS WE CAN DESTROY HIM IF WE ALL FIRE OUR RINGS TOGETHER AND WRAP HIS ASS IN A TECHNICOLOR DREAMCOAT!
ALLOW ME TO GIVE YOU ALL SOME BREATHING ROOM TO TAKE DOWN THAT MONSTROSITY.
CONNECTION SEVERED.
CONNECTION SEVERED.
CONNECTION SEVERED.
CONNECTION SEVERED.
CONNECTION SEVERED.
NOW DOVE'S THE BEST BUG ZAPPER I'VE EVER SEEN!

LET'S LIGHT UP THIS SON OF A BITCH LIKE A CHRISTMAS TREE!
RARGHHHH!
IF THIS IS ALL YOU HAVE, YOUR TRIVIAL EXISTENCE IS FINALLY ABOUT TO COME TO AN END!
MUNK, WHY DIDN'T THE MERGING OF OUR ENERGY BEAMS OBLITERATE THE ANTI-MONITOR LIKE IT DID OTHER BLACK LANTERNS?
ALL READINGS INDICATE THAT THE ANTI-MONITOR HAS NOT FULLY TRANSFORMED INTO A BLACK LANTERN AT THIS JUNCTURE.
CRAP. I KNEW IT WAS TOO GOOD TO BE TRUE.
THEN WE NEED TO KEEP HIM DISTRACTED-- UNFOCUSED--SO WE CAN--

IOLANDE! LOOK--
--OUTAAARGGHH!
UNN!
ZZZRAAAKKK
VATH! NO!
YOU'RE WOUNDED, VATH! WE HAVE TO GET YOU OUT OF HERE!
C'MON, DAMN IT! YOU CAN'T DO ANY GOOD UP HERE!
SCREW THAT! MY LEGS ARE CAUTERIZED-- DON'T TAKE ME OUTTA THIS, ISAMOT!
IF MY NUMBER'S UP TODAY, I'M GOING DOWN FACE FORWARD-- NOT ON MY BACK!

CONNECTION SEVERED.
AAAAIIEEEE!
THIS CITY WILL BURN!
ONCE I FREE MYSELF FROM THIS ABERRATION THIS WHOLE WORLD WILL FINALLY BURN!
CONNECTION SEVERED.
CONNECTION SEVERED.
FASCINATING.
THIS POWER OF YOURS TO DESTROY BLACK LANTERNS, WHERE DOES IT COME FROM?
I'M NOT SURE. I HAVE NO IDEA WHAT I'M CONNECTED TO AND WHY IT'S SINGLED ME OUT.
IF YOU ARE WILLING TO UNDERTAKE A PERILOUS ENDEAVOR, I DO BELIEVE WE CAN STOP THE ANTI-MONITOR.
I'LL DO WHATEVER I CAN.
THIS BLACK BATTERY WILL NOT HOLD ME FOREVER!
ARE YOU READY, DOVE?
YES, I AM.
OKAY, GUY, WE'RE SET AT THIS END--
--DO IT!

AWRIGHT, YA RED BASTARDS--
--DRENCH HIM!
YAAARGHHH!
NOW, BEDOVIAN, WHILE HE'S BLINDED--

--TAKE THE SHOT!
KIKKIKIKIKIKIKI
BLAMM
CHARGE HER UP!
SHWOOOOSHH
ZZZRRRAP
LET'S HOPE HIS AIM IS TRUE!

RRRAAAGGHH!

UGGGNNNN!
A HEAD SHOT! CLEAN THROUGH!
DID IT STOP HIM?
YOU BETCHA! HE'S DOWN AND--
NO! IT'S CUT OUR ENERGY TETHERS!
THE BLACK BATTERY'S GOT HIM!
THEN WHAT ARE WE WAITING FOR...

WHAT THE HELL--
IT DIDN'T WORK! WE COULDN'T GET HIM OUT ALL THE WAY!
THE DAMN BATTERY'S STILL SUCKIN' JUICE FROM HIM!
THE ANTI-MONITOR'S BEING PULLED BACK IN!
AB HIM!

...LET'S BRING THE PAIN TO NEKRON!

GREEN LANTERN CORPS 47
Cover by Patrick Gleason and
Christian Alamy with Randy Mayor

GOODBYE DARKNESS

PATRICK GLEASON
PENCILS

REBECCA BUCHMAN
TOM NGUYEN
KEITH CHAMPAGNE
MARK IRWIN
INKS

LET'S POWER THIS **BAD BOY** UP!

LET'S!

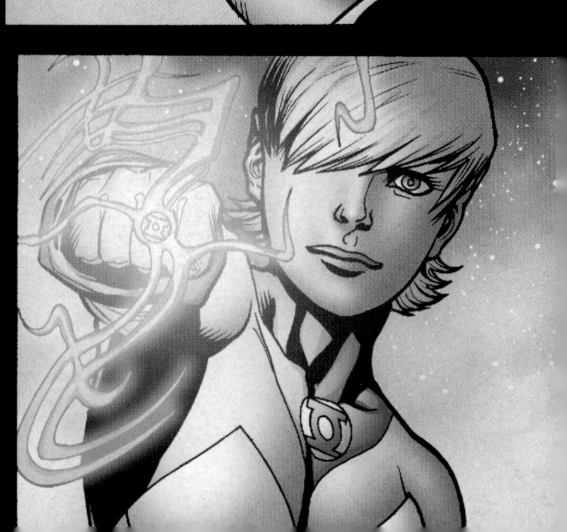

THE PLANET OA, SECTOR 0.
HOME TO THE GUARDIANS OF THE UNIVERSE AND...
...THE
GREEN LANTERN
CORPS

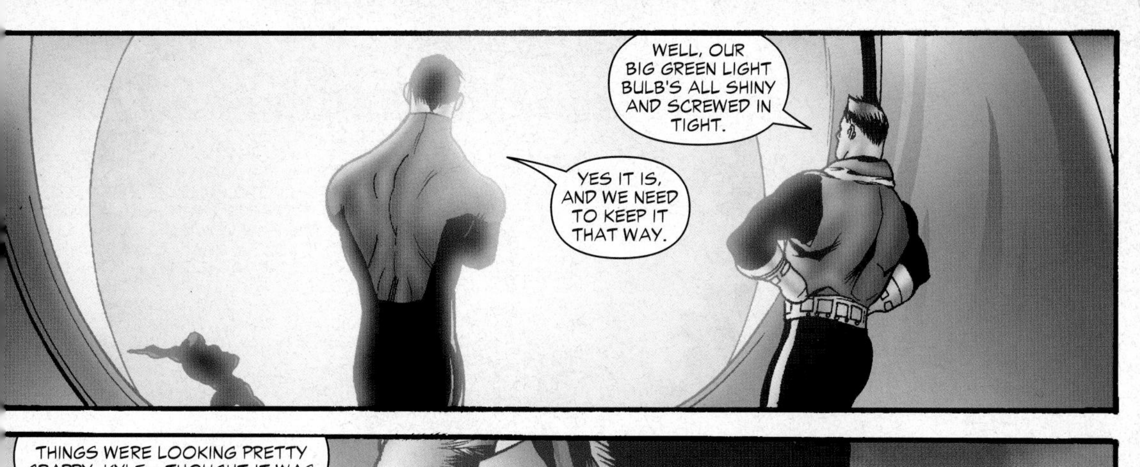

WELL, OUR BIG GREEN LIGHT BULB'S ALL SHINY AND SCREWED IN TIGHT.
YES IT IS, AND WE NEED TO KEEP IT THAT WAY.

THINGS WERE LOOKING PRETTY CRAPPY, KYLE-- THOUGHT IT WAS "STICK A FORK IN OUR ASS WE'RE DONE" TIME.
YEAH... IT DIDN'T LOOK GOOD, GUY.

WITH YOU PULLING THAT *KAMIKAZE* MOVE ON THOSE BLACK LANTERNS--DYING AND ALL--I WAS DEFINITELY GETTING THAT *LITTLE BIG HORN* VIBE.
WELL, WATCHING YOU PUKE OUT NAPALM, BURNING EVERYTHING IN SIGHT, AND GETTING READY TO *KILL US* WASN'T EXACTLY MAKING ME FEEL TOO OPTIMISTIC ABOUT OUR CHANCES EITHER.

BUT WE PULLED IT TOGETHER AND SHUT THE *BAD MAN* DOWN.
AND THE *PRICE* TO DO THAT SEEMS TO KEEP RISING.
ALL WE'VE BEEN DOING IS PUTTING OA BACK TOGETHER EVERY OTHER DAY AND BURYING OUR DEAD.

IT'S DEJA VU ALL OVER AGAIN, BUDDY.
WHAT DO YOU MEAN?
THIS ROLLERCOASTER HASN'T STOPPED SINCE WE SLAPPED SINESTRO AND HIS CORPS OF YELLOW SNOTS AND PUT THE STATUE OF LIBERTY AND HALF OF NEW YORK BACK UP, WATCHED THE SCIENCELLS EXPLODE INTO A FULL RIOT, HAD THE PROTECTIVE SHELL AROUND OA GET OBLITERATED AND RAIN DOWN ON US AND THEN, TO TOP IT ALL OFF, FOUGHT A GAZILLION OF NEKRON'S BLACK LANTERN COCKROACHES TO THE DEATH AS THEY TRIED TO SUCK OUR CENTRAL BATTERY DRY AND DESTROY NOT ONLY THE EARTH BUT THE WHOLE UNIVERSE, NOT TO MENTION A BUNCHA LANTERNS STILL UNACCOUNTED FOR.
DID I LEAVE ANYTHING OUT?
ONLY THAT WHEN THE GOING GETS TOUGH, THE TOUGH GET GOING.
I SURE AS HELL DIDN'T APPRECIATE THAT THE BLUE BELLS SEEM TO BE AT THE CENTER OF A LOTTA OUR MISERY THIS GO ROUND.
I'M FEELING BETTER KNOWING THAT GANTHET'S BACK AND GOING TO BE AROUND MORE.
SCAR TURNED OUT TO BE A REAL BAG O' FUN.
YEAH, GANTHET AS A DEPUTY LANTERN. LIVE LONG ENOUGH, YA GET TO SEE EVERYTHING.
I LIKE IT WHEN THE GENERALS GET DIRTY IN THE TRENCHES ONCE IN A WHILE--KEEPS 'EM HONEST.
YOU HOPE.
YEP. THAT'S ALL WE CAN DO, PAL.

GREETINGS TO ALL OF YOU GATHERED HERE TODAY.
AS YOU KNOW, DEEP WITHIN MY CORE IS ALL THAT REMAINS OF OUR HONORED LANTERN DEAD.
AFTER MUCH DELIBERATION WITH LANTERN MORRO, THE KEEPER OF THE CRYPT...
...WE CAN THINK OF NO GREATER WAY TO PAY TRIBUTE TO THEIR STRENGTH, DIGNITY, PRINCIPLES OF JUSTICE...
...AND OF COURSE ULTIMATE SACRIFICE...

...THAN WITH A MEMORIAL OF LIFE.

THESE LEAVES OF GREEN WILL NEVER BE BLOWN AWAY.
THIS TREE WILL NEVER COME DOWN.
...JUST LIKE THE CORPS!
IT'S A PERENNIAL.
JUST LIKE US...
SODAM SHOULD BE UP THERE ON ONE OF THOSE BRANCHES...
...HE SACRIFICED EVERYTHING...SITTING IN THE MIDDLE OF THAT DAXAM SUN...
...WHAT ABOUT KEEPING HIS MEMORY ALIVE...
...I KNOW THIS SOUNDS CRAZY, BUT JUST BECAUSE YOU'RE ALIVE DOESN'T MEAN YOU'RE REALLY ALIVE.
NOTHING CRAZY ABOUT THAT, ARISIA. I KNOW WHAT YOU MEAN.
THEY SHOULD BE HERE.
WHO?
THE GUARDIANS, THAT'S WHO.
INSTEAD OF FLOATING AROUND IN THE CITADEL, THEY SHOULD BE WITH US HERE--PAYING THEIR RESPECTS.
THIS ETERNAL FLAME WILL BURN FOR AS LONG AS THERE IS AT LEAST ONE GREEN LANTERN RING SHINING SOMEWHERE IN THIS VAST UNIVERSE.

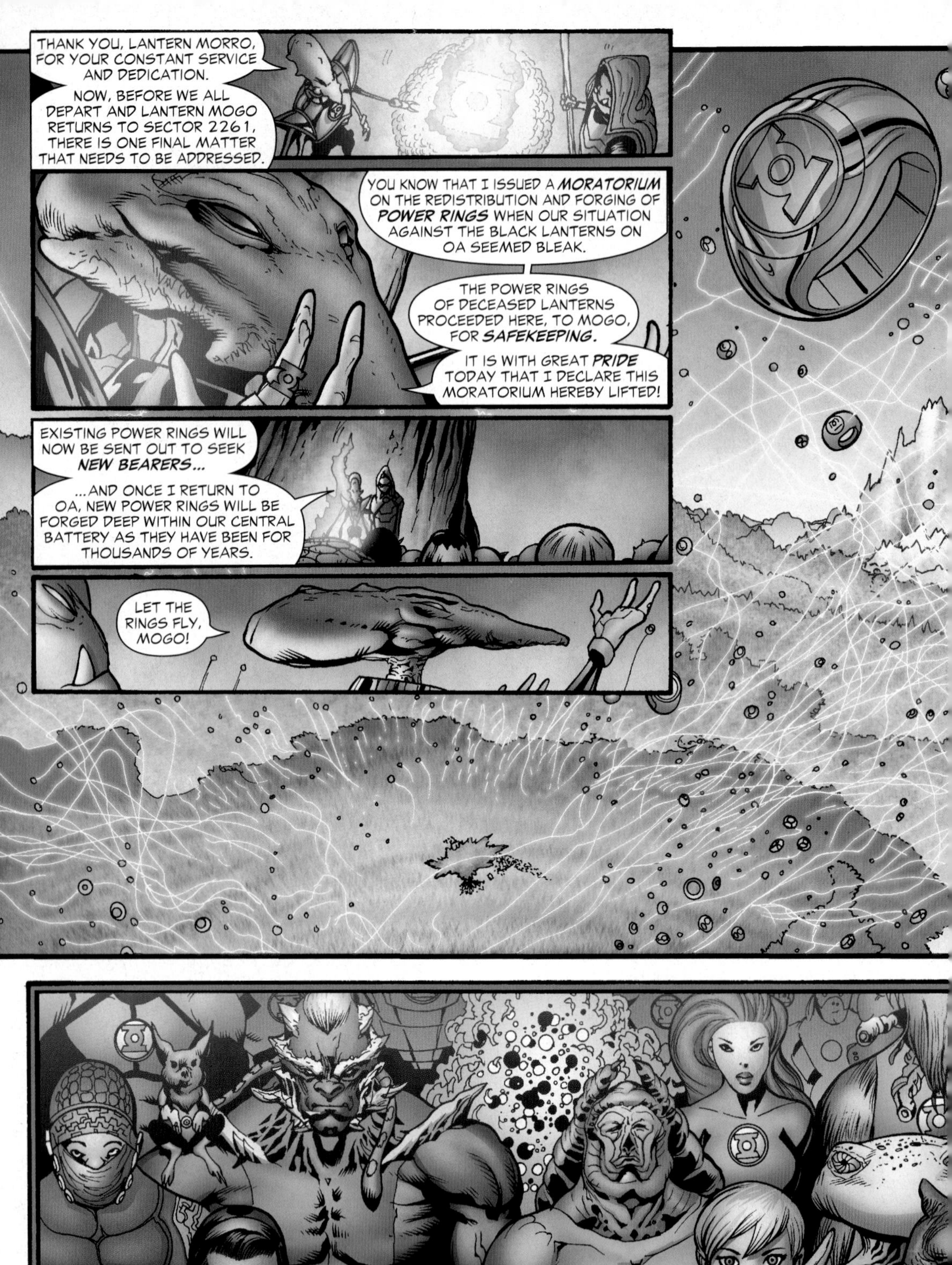
THANK YOU, LANTERN MORRO, FOR YOUR CONSTANT SERVICE AND DEDICATION.
NOW, BEFORE WE ALL DEPART AND LANTERN MOGO RETURNS TO SECTOR 2261, THERE IS ONE FINAL MATTER THAT NEEDS TO BE ADDRESSED.
YOU KNOW THAT I ISSUED A MORATORIUM ON THE REDISTRIBUTION AND FORGING OF POWER RINGS WHEN OUR SITUATION AGAINST THE BLACK LANTERNS ON OA SEEMED BLEAK.
THE POWER RINGS OF DECEASED LANTERNS PROCEEDED HERE, TO MOGO, FOR SAFEKEEPING.
IT IS WITH GREAT PRIDE TODAY THAT I DECLARE THIS MORATORIUM HEREBY LIFTED!
EXISTING POWER RINGS WILL NOW BE SENT OUT TO SEEK NEW BEARERS...
...AND ONCE I RETURN TO OA, NEW POWER RINGS WILL BE FORGED DEEP WITHIN OUR CENTRAL BATTERY AS THEY HAVE BEEN FOR THOUSANDS OF YEARS.
LET THE RINGS FLY, MOGO!

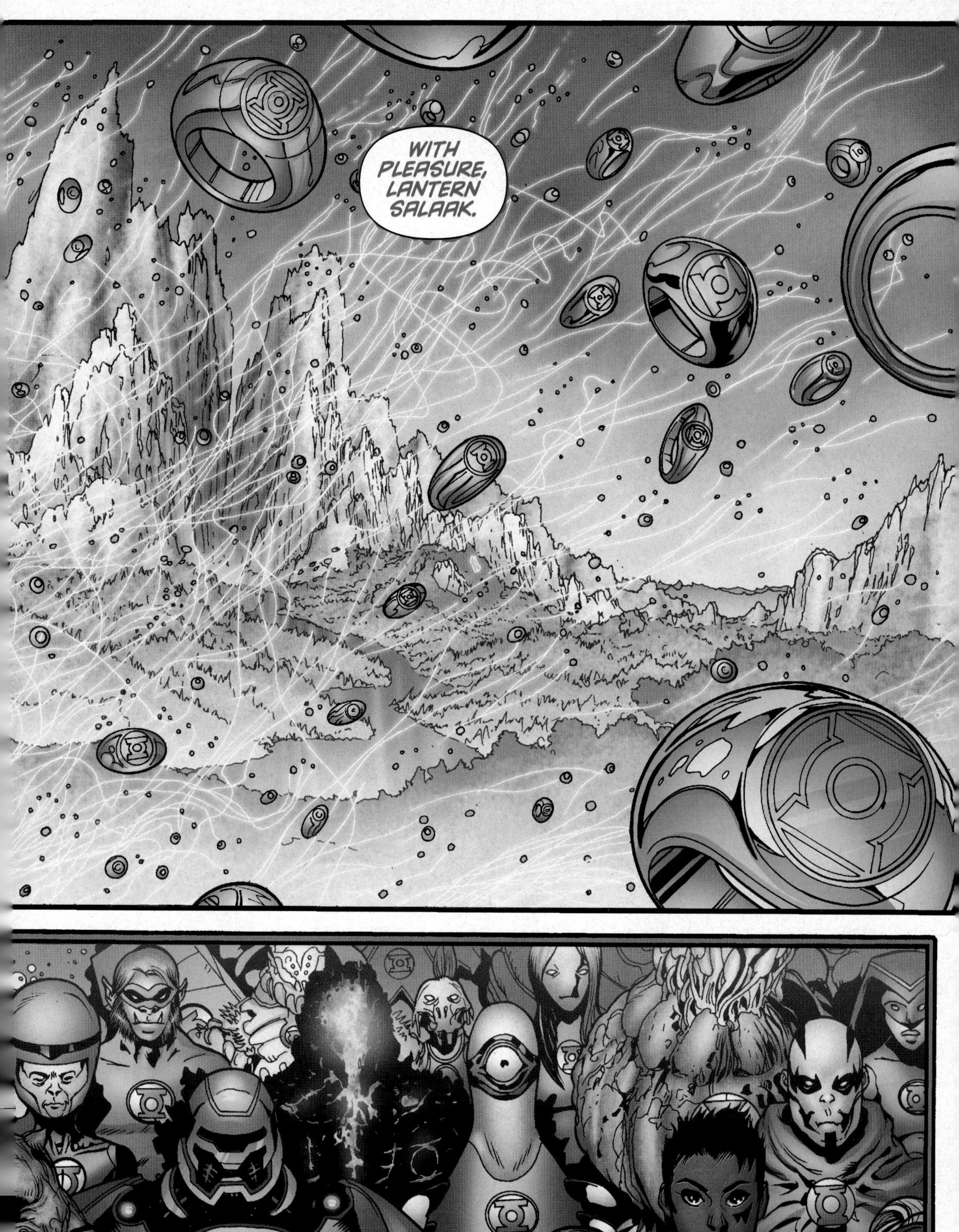
WITH PLEASURE, LANTERN SALAAK.

OA.
IT'S BROKEN, SORA...
...NOT MUCH LEFT.
A HISTORY OF THE CORPS WAS A GOOD IDEA.
A PERFECT OUTLET FOR YOU, KYLE.
YEAH, IT WAS.
I BARELY GOT A CHANCE TO START THE DAMN THING AND HERE IT IS AT OUR FEET ALREADY.
GUESS PROCRASTINATION HAS ITS MERITS AFTER ALL.
I WOULDN'T EXACTLY DEFINE YOUR PARTICIPATION IN A WAR OF LIGHT AS PROCRASTINATION, KYLE.
WELL, WHATEVER IT WAS, THE MURAL'S GOING TO HAVE TO WAIT. THERE'S A LOT OF REBUILDING WAITING TO GET DONE AND--
WHY DOES IT HAVE TO WAIT?
GET A NEW RECRUIT QUARTERS UP AND TAILOR THE FACADE FOR THE MURAL THIS TIME--PRIORITIZE IT--START OVER.

FROM SCRATCH, HUH?
YES, FROM SCRATCH.
YOU WERE DOING BEAUTIFUL WORK, KYLE.
GUY SAID SOMETHING ONCE ABOUT EVERYBODY HAVING TO LEAVE SOME BLOOD ON THE FLOOR...
WHAT DID HE MEAN?
I THINK HE MEANT THE ONLY WAY YOU CAN REALLY EARN SOMETHING YOU CARE ABOUT IS TO FIGHT FOR IT.
WELL, WE'VE ALL DONE PLENTY OF THAT, DON'T YOU THINK?
ABSOLUTELY. I THINK WE ALL NEED A FRESH COAT OF PRIMER AROUND HERE.
REMEMBER, YOU STARTED THIS MURAL FOR A REASON, KYLE.
WE'RE ALL GOING TO NEED A MORALE BOOST AND A REMINDER OF THE CORPS' PROUD HISTORY AND THE FUTURE WE'RE FIGHTING FOR--THE NEW RECRUITS MOST OF ALL.
YOU NEED IT. I NEED IT. THE CORPS NEEDS IT.
I SWORE TO YOU I'D NEVER LET YOU DOWN , SORA.
AND IF YOU DO, I'LL BE THE FIRST TO LET YOU KNOW, KYLE.

OUR NEW RECRUITS WILL BE ARRIVING SHORTLY, KILOWOG.
I AM UPLOADING THEIR PROFILES TO YOUR RING SO YOU CAN ACQUAINT YOURSELF WITH--
NO.
NO?
NO.
WHAT EXACTLY IS YOUR NO REFERRING TO?
IT'S TIME FOR A CHANGE, SALAAK.
MAY I ASK WHAT KIND OF CHANGE?
TO JUST BEING A LANTERN AGAIN.
SINCE WHEN DID YOU STOP BEING ONE?
I'VE TRAINED AND BURIED MORE LANTERN RECRUITS IN THE LAST 2 YEARS THAN I HAVE SINCE I BECAME A DRILL INSTRUCTOR 20 YEARS AGO.
YES, YOU MAY HAVE BURIED MANY RECRUITS OVER THE YEARS, KILOWOG, BUT BECAUSE OF YOUR TRAINING AND DISCIPLINE YOU'VE SAVED PROBABLY TEN TIMES THAT NUMBER.
COUNTLESS RECRUITS OWE YOU THEIR LIVES FOR WHAT YOU--
THEY DON'T OWE ME ANYTHING, SALAAK...BUT I OWE MYSELF SOMETHING RIGHT NOW...
...SO I'M DECLINING THE DRILL INSTRUCTOR DUTY AT THIS TIME.
HURRM.

BEFORE YOU MAKE A *FINAL* DECISION, MIGHT I SUGGEST YOU TAKE A FEW DAYS TO--
I'VE TAKEN *MORE* THAN A FEW DAYS TO REACH THIS CONCLUSION.
I JUST WANT-- *NEED*--TO BE A SPACE COP AGAIN.

I SEE...
SO, HOW WOULD YOU LIKE ME TO ENTER... *THIS* ON THE RECORD?
YOU CAN PUT IT DOWN AS A REQUEST FOR LEAVE OF ABSENCE FROM D.I. DUTY.
TAK
TAK
TAK
TAK
TAK
TAK
TAK

YOUR D.I. STATUS HAS BEEN CHANGED, AND YOUR LEAVE OF ABSENCE IS HEREBY GRANTED.
YOU ARE, AS OF THIS MOMENT, *SIMPLY* A LANTERN.
C'MON, SALAAK, I CAN HEAR THAT TONE IN YOUR--
I *DO NOT* AGREE WITH YOUR DECISION, LANTERN KILOWOG, BUT I MUST RESPECT IT.
NOW, IF YOU WILL EXCUSE ME, I HAVE A *PRESSING* NEED TO LOCATE A QUALIFIED D.I. FOR THE NEW CLASS OF RECRUITS THAT WILL SOON BE--
RELAX, SALAAK, DID YOU THINK I WAS GONNA PUT LANTERN RECRUITS INTO THE HANDS OF JUST ANYBODY?
I'VE REACHED OUT TO SOMEONE I TRUST COMPLETELY.
IS THAT RIGHT? AND JUST *WHO* DO YOU HAVE IN MIND?

HELLO, SALAAK.
AH, *LANTERN STEL.*
SO, THE BATON HAS BEEN PASSED.
I'D BE MORE THAN HAPPY TO WHIP THE NEW RECRUITS INTO SHAPE UNTIL WOG HERE WANTS HIS JOB BACK.

UURRRRMM...
WAKEY WAKEY.
...WHAT THE HELL?
HOW DO YOU LIKE 'EM, VATH?
LIKE 'EM-- WHAT, IS THIS SOME KINDA JOKE?
JOKE?
NO WAY, BUDDY--THEY'RE A GIFT.
GIFT?!?
ACK!
YOU THINK THIS IS A GIFT?!?
KRAAK

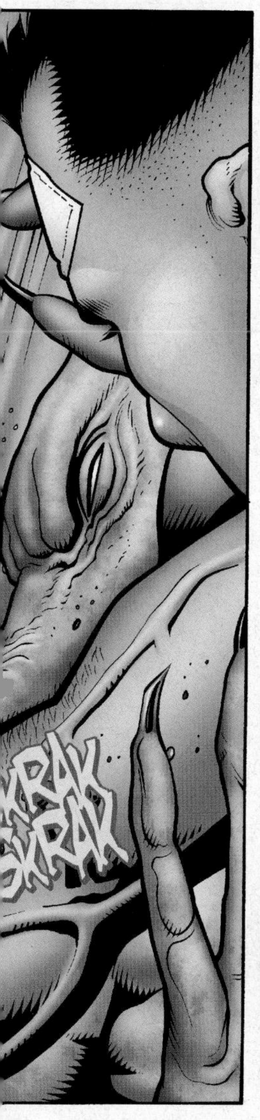
KRAK
KRAK

WHAT DID YOU DO TO ME, ISAMOT?!
DO TO YOU?
I GAVE YOU MY LEGS, VATH.

I DIDN'T ASK FOR THEM!
YOU DIDN'T HAVE TO.
WHAT THE HELL MADE YOU THINK I'D WANT TO WALK AROUND WITH...WITH... THESE FOR THE REST OF MY DAMN LIFE?!?

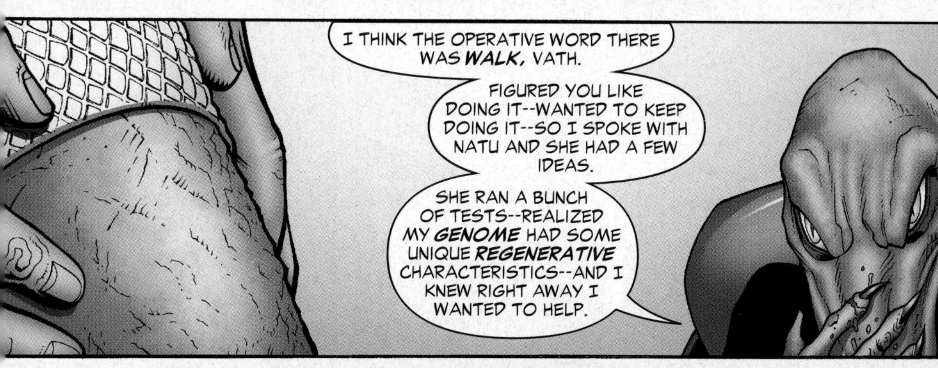
I THINK THE OPERATIVE WORD THERE WAS WALK, VATH.
FIGURED YOU LIKE DOING IT--WANTED TO KEEP DOING IT--SO I SPOKE WITH NATU AND SHE HAD A FEW IDEAS.
SHE RAN A BUNCH OF TESTS--REALIZED MY GENOME HAD SOME UNIQUE REGENERATIVE CHARACTERISTICS--AND I KNEW RIGHT AWAY I WANTED TO HELP.

HELP WHAT?
HELP ME LOOK LIKE A THANAGARIAN?!?

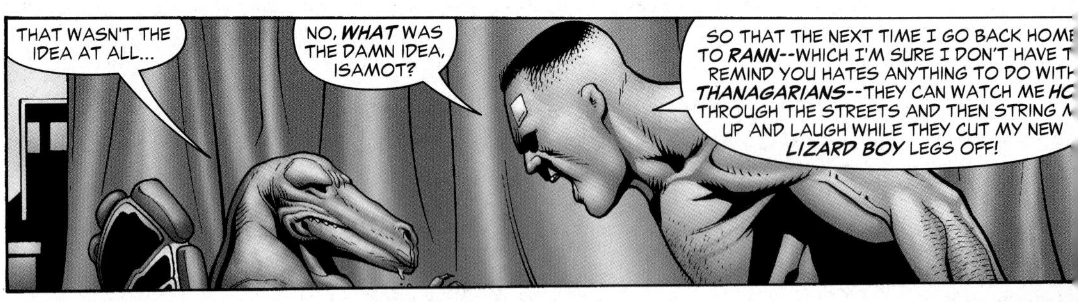
THAT WASN'T THE IDEA AT ALL...
NO, WHAT WAS THE DAMN IDEA, ISAMOT?
SO THAT THE NEXT TIME I GO BACK HOME TO RANN--WHICH I'M SURE I DON'T HAVE T REMIND YOU HATES ANYTHING TO DO WITH THANAGARIANS--THEY CAN WATCH ME HO THROUGH THE STREETS AND THEN STRING UP AND LAUGH WHILE THEY CUT MY NEW LIZARD BOY LEGS OFF!

VATH... I THOUGHT THAT--
NO, THAT'S ONE THING YOU DIDN'T DO WAS THINK.

LOOK AT ME!
WHY DID YOU DO THIS TO ME?!?
YOU WANT TO KNOW WHY I DID THIS?!

SKRAK
WHY I CHOPPED MY OWN DAMN LEGS OFF?!?

BECAUSE I THOUGHT YOU'D DO THE SAME FOR ME!
BECAUSE WE'VE ALWAYS GOT EACH OTHER'S BACK!
BECAUSE WE'RE LANTERNS!
BECAUSE WE'RE SUPPOSED TO BE PARTNERS!

YOU DON'T WANT MY LEGS--SAY THE WORD!
I'LL SLICE THEM RIGHT OFF, YOU UNGRATEFUL SON OF A BITCH!

ENOUGH!
UNNF!
URRR!
I CAME TO SEE HOW YOU BOTH ARE DOING, AND THIS IS HOW YOU'RE TREATING EACH OTHER?
YOU'VE RISKED YOUR LIVES FOR EACH OTHER. YOU'VE RISKED YOUR LIVES FOR ME.
YOU SHOULD BE ASHAMED OF YOURSELVES.
C'MON, GET THE HELL UP.
RRR...
...MAYBE I'LL GET USED TO THESE CRAZY ASS LEGS EVENTUALLY.
BUT I DOUBT IT.
LET'S GO GET SOME LUNCH BEFORE YOU TWO KILL EACH OTHER.

THE PLANETARY CITADEL.
SALAAK, WE WANT A MEET WITH THE BLUES.
THEY ARE NOT TO BE DISTURBED, GARDNER.
I WILL GLADLY SCHEDULE ANOTHER MEETING FOR--
NOW, SALAAK-- DOES *NOW* WORK FOR THEM?
ACTUALLY, NO, IT DOES NOT.
WE'VE SCHEDULED TWO MEETINGS AND THEY'VE *CANCELLED* BOTH.
AS I SAID, I WILL--
WELL, *NOW* WORKS FOR US!
RAYNER, THEIR SCHEDULE IS--
I DON'T GIVE A DAMN ABOUT *THEIR* SCHEDULE, SALAAK...
BOO

...THEY'RE ON *OURS* FOR THE NEXT TEN MINUTES.

WHY ARE WE BEING DISTURBED AT THIS TIME?
LANTERNS GARDNER, RAYNER AND ARISIA DEMAND TO--
DEMAND?
THERE ARE NO DEMANDS MADE OF OUR TIME.
WE REQUESTED TO MEET WITH YOU AND--
AND THOSE REQUESTS WERE NOT HONORED DUE TO CIRCUMSTANCES BEYOND OUR CONTROL.
WE WILL GLADLY ENTERTAIN YOUR THOUGHTS AT A--
ENTERTAIN THIS!
KRAKKK
ARISIA!

YOU DARE STRIKE A GUARDIAN?
THAT WAS FOR SODAM!
WHEN HE NEEDED YOU MOST, YOU LEFT HIM DEFENSELESS AGAINST MONGUL!
ARISIA! DIAL IT DOWN!
WHAT ARE YOU TALKING ABOUT, LANTERN ARISIA?
WE WERE NEVER CONTACTED BY LANTERN YAT.
YOU DENIED HIM ACCESS TO TAP INTO HIS ION POWER WHEN WE WERE ON DAXAM!
THE ONLY WAY SODAM COULD SAVE DAXAM FROM MONGUL WAS TO GIVE THE PEOPLE OF DAXAM ENHANCED POWERS BY CHANGING ITS RED SUN TO YELLOW--
--AND THE ONLY WAY HE CO DO THAT AFTER YOU DEN HIM ACCESS WAS TO REM HIS RING AND JUMPSTART ION POWER WITH A MASS ENERGY SURGE BY SACRIFICING HIMSELF INSIDE THEIR SUN.
THAT WAS GUARDIAN SCAR'S DOING.
UNBEKNOWNST TO US AT THAT TIME, SHE WAS MANIPULATING SEVERAL FACETS OF THE CORPS TO SERVE NEKRON'S NEFARIOUS PLANS.
SCAR PAID FOR HER CRIMES.
YEAH, WELL, NOT ONLY WAS THERE A LOTTA CRAP THAT WAS UNBEKNOWNST TO ALL OF YA...
...THERE WAS A HELLUVA BUNCH OF THINGS YOU DID THAT SUBVERTED EVERYTHING THE CORPS STANDS FOR...
...LIKE CREATING THOSE POWER-HUNGRY ALPHA LANTERNS, WHACKING ALL THOSE UNARMED SCIENCELL PRISONERS AND--
THE THIRD LAW.

WHAT ABOUT THE THIRD LAW, LANTERN RAYNER?
PHYSICAL RELATIONSHIPS AND LOVE BETWEEN MEMBERS OF THE GREEN LANTERN CORPS IS FORBIDDEN.
YES, WE ARE QUITE FAMILIAR WITH ITS WORDING. WE WROTE IT.
YOU SAW ALL THE POWER RINGS THAT WERE RETURNED TO OA BY VETERAN LANTERNS UNWILLING TO LIVE BY THAT PRONOUNCEMENT.
LANTERNS WITH INVALUABLE EXPERIENCE AND KNOWLEDGE--LANTERNS WHO'VE MADE THE CORPS AS STRONG AS IT IS TODAY NOT BECAUSE OF THEIR INTIMATE RELATIONSHIP WITH ANOTHER LANTERN, BUT SIMPLY BECAUSE OF THEIR DEVOTION AND DUTY TO THE CAUSE...
...AND TO THE OATH THAT COMES WITH THE RING.
I'M AFRAID A LOT MORE'RE GOING TO RESIGN IF YOU DO NOT REPEAL THE THIRD LAW.
AND JUST WHY WOULD WE REPEAL IT, LANTERN RAYNER?
BECAUSE IT'S WRONG.
BECAUSE IF YOU TAKE AWAY THE HEART OF A LANTERN, YOU'RE LEFT WITH AN UNTHINKING AND UNCARING AUTOMATED SHELL--THAT'S WHY.
YEAH, AND WE ALL KNOW HOW GREAT THAT'S TURNED OUT FOR YA IN THE PAST --COUGH-- MANHUNTERS--COUGH-- ALPHA LANTERNS.
WITH RESPECT, COLD, EMOTIONLESS LOGIC DIDN'T WIN THIS WAR OF LIGHT AND BEAT BACK THE BLACKEST NIGHT PROPHECY.
LANTERNS WITH HEART DID.
LANTERNS WITH SOUL DID.
AND LANTERNS WITH WILL WON IT AND SAVED THE UNIVERSE.
WHEN YOU ALL FINALLY REALIZE-- AND EMBRACE THAT FACT--THAT'S WHEN THIS CORPS WILL FULLY BE ON THE RIGHT TRACK.

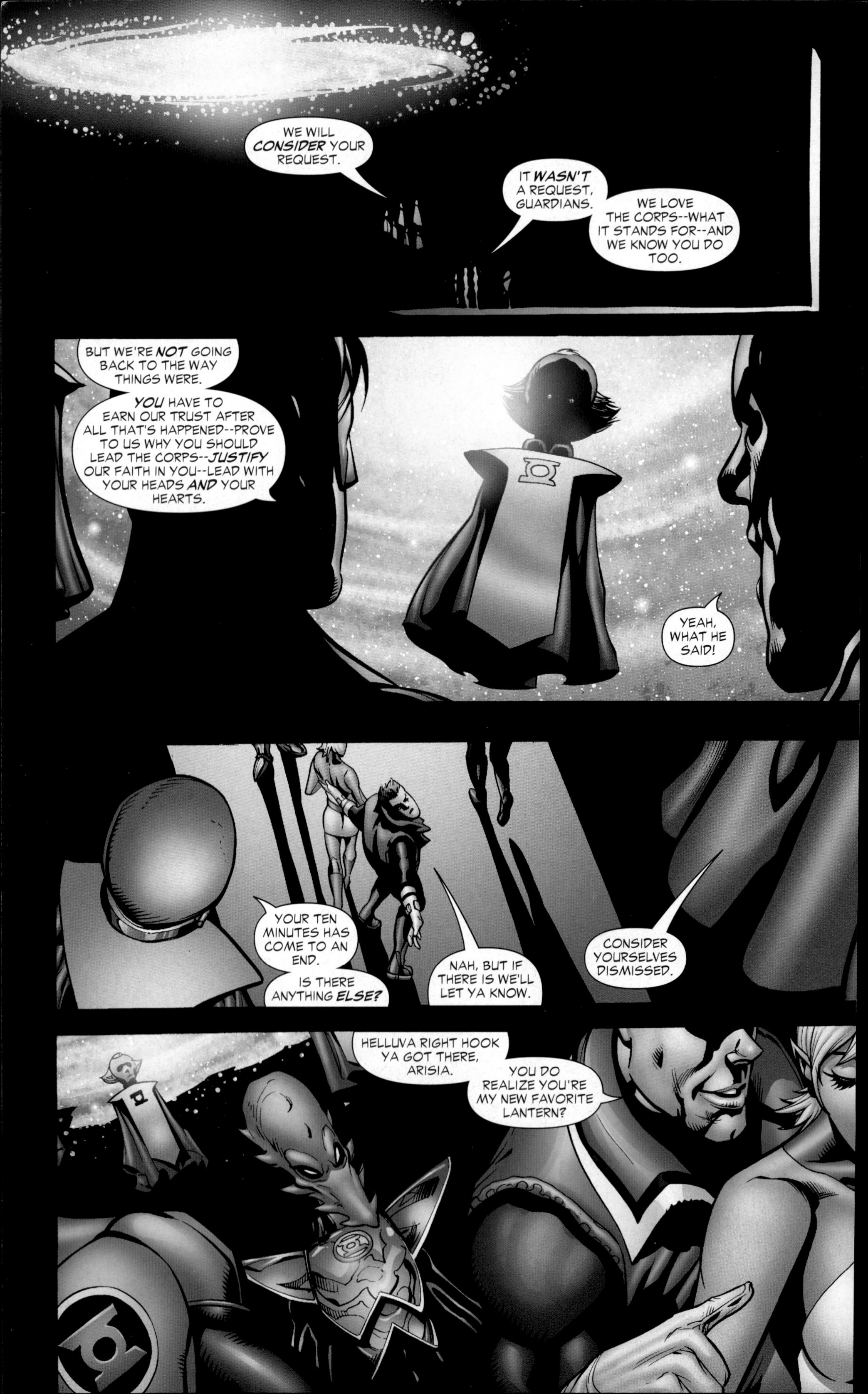
WE WILL CONSIDER YOUR REQUEST.
IT WASN'T A REQUEST, GUARDIANS.
WE LOVE THE CORPS--WHAT IT STANDS FOR--AND WE KNOW YOU DO TOO.
BUT WE'RE NOT GOING BACK TO THE WAY THINGS WERE.
YOU HAVE TO EARN OUR TRUST AFTER ALL THAT'S HAPPENED--PROVE TO US WHY YOU SHOULD LEAD THE CORPS--JUSTIFY OUR FAITH IN YOU--LEAD WITH YOUR HEADS AND YOUR HEARTS.
YEAH, WHAT HE SAID!
YOUR TEN MINUTES HAS COME TO AN END.
IS THERE ANYTHING ELSE?
NAH, BUT IF THERE IS WE'LL LET YA KNOW.
CONSIDER YOURSELVES DISMISSED.
HELLUVA RIGHT HOOK YA GOT THERE, ARISIA.
YOU DO REALIZE YOU'RE MY NEW FAVORITE LANTERN?

SALAAK, IT APPEARS THAT THE LINE OF DISTINCTION IS BEGINNING TO BLUR BETWEEN US AND THE LANTERN CORPS.
IT IS IMPERATIVE THAT YOU MAINTAIN--
WITH ALL DUE RESPECT, GUARDIANS, I WILL MAINTAIN NOTHING.
WITHOUT A DOUBT, I AM HERE TO SERVE AT THE GUARDIANS' PLEASURE.
I AM HERE BECAUSE I WANT TO BE HERE.
BECAUSE I BELIEVE IN WHAT YOU HAVE ALL DEVOTED YOURSELVES TO...
...WHAT I HAVE DEVOTED MYSELF TO.
BUT I AM NOT A PUPPET, NOR AN ERRAND BOY.
I WILL HAVE QUESTIONS.
QUESTIONS ABOUT POLICY AND DIRECTIVES THAT THIS COUNCIL WILL MAKE.
BY SERVING YOU, I SERVE THE CORPS...
...AND WITH THAT RESPONSIBILITY I AM OBLIGED TO APPLY TRUTH TO POWER WHEN I DEEM IT NECESSARY.

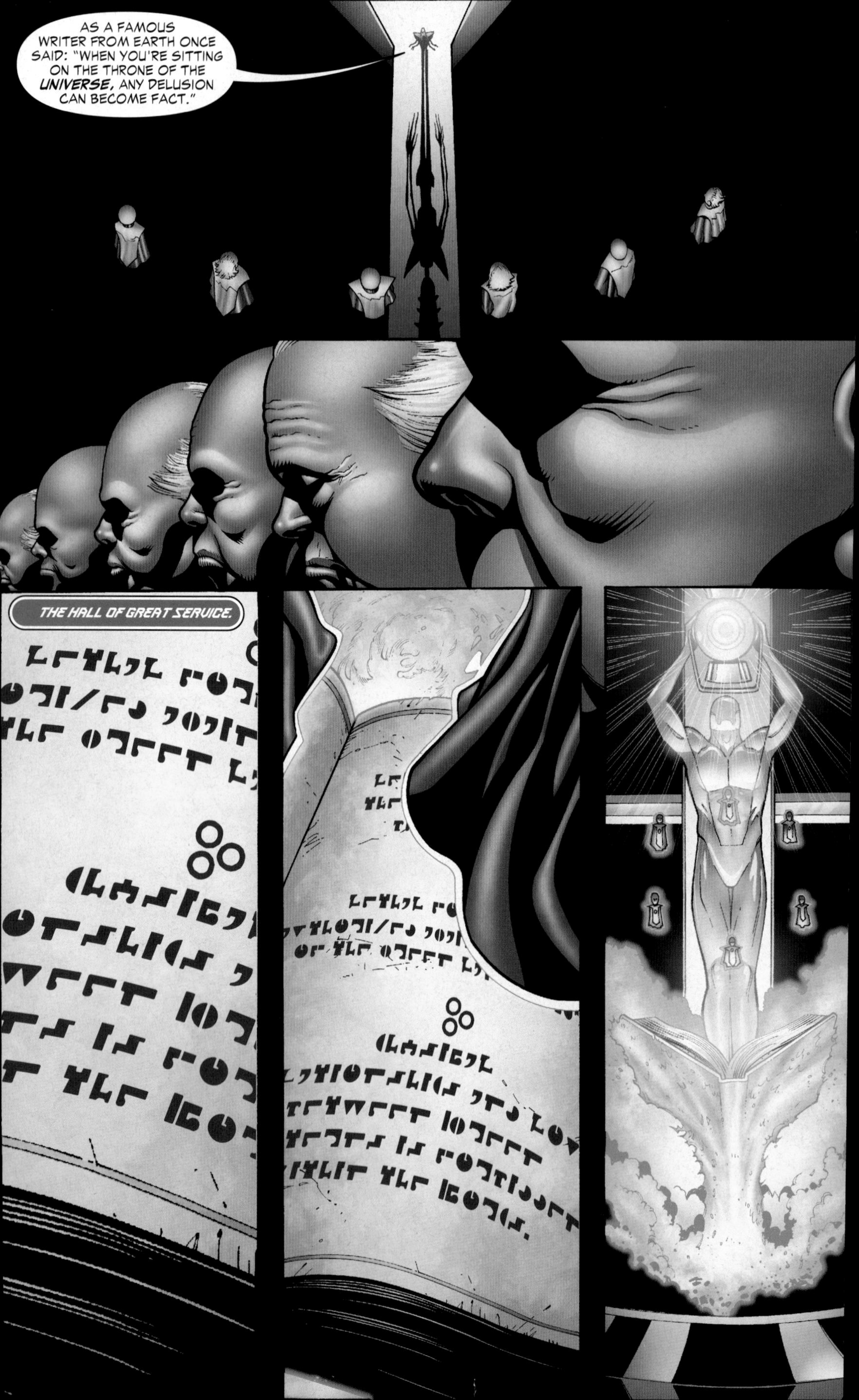
AS A FAMOUS WRITER FROM EARTH ONCE SAID: "WHEN YOU'RE SITTING ON THE THRONE OF THE UNIVERSE, ANY DELUSION CAN BECOME FACT."
THE HALL OF GREAT SERVICE.

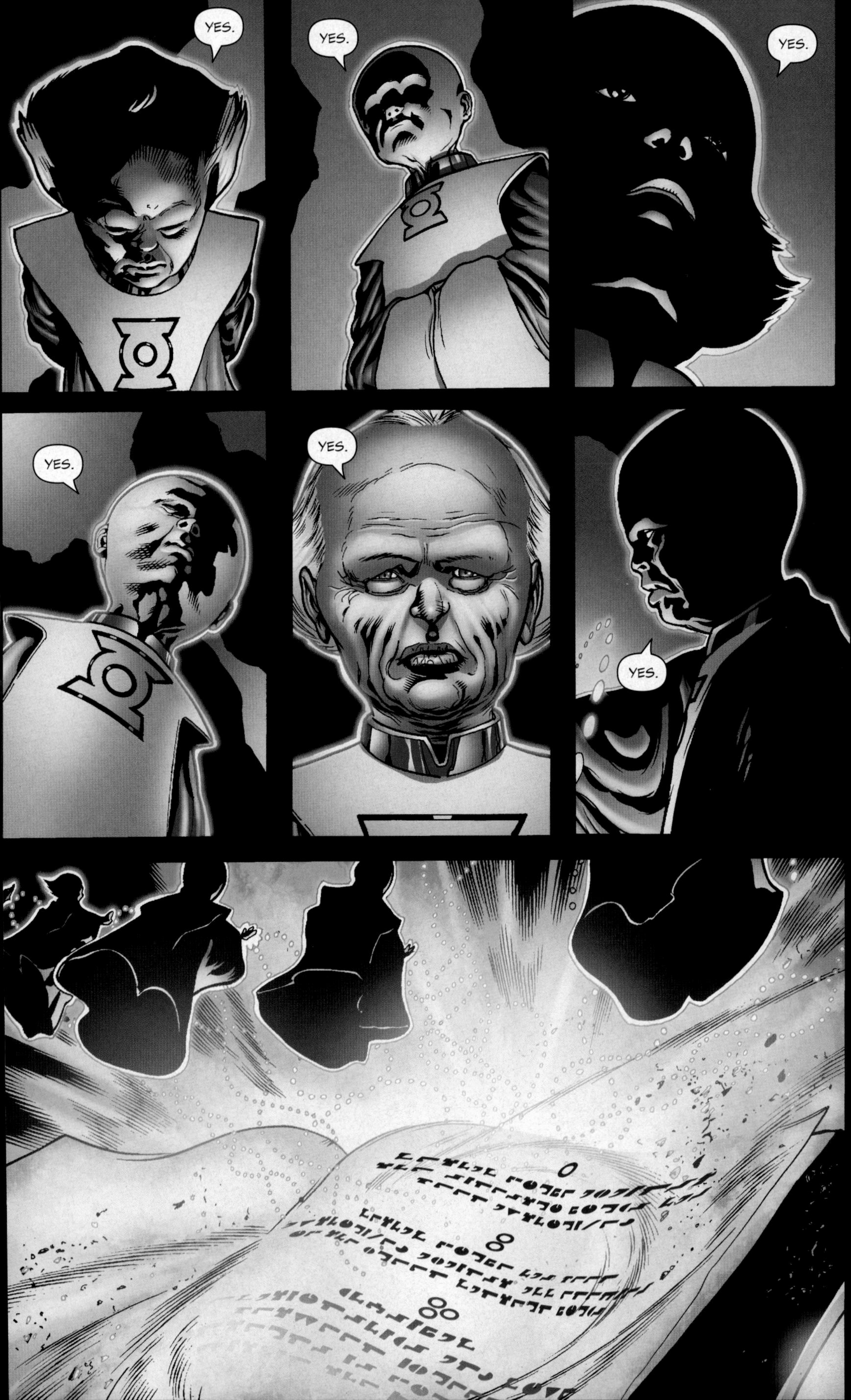

YES.
YES.
YES.
YES.
YES.
YES.

THEY BROKE THE BAR!

THEY BROKE THE WHOLE #$$% BAR!

HEY, IT WAS ONE OF YOUR BETTER IDEAS, GUY.
A GREAT PLACE FOR YOU TO HAVE YOUR THREE-RING CIRCUS AND KEEP EVERYONE SMILING AND ENTERTAINED.
YEAH. SURE WAS, KYLE.

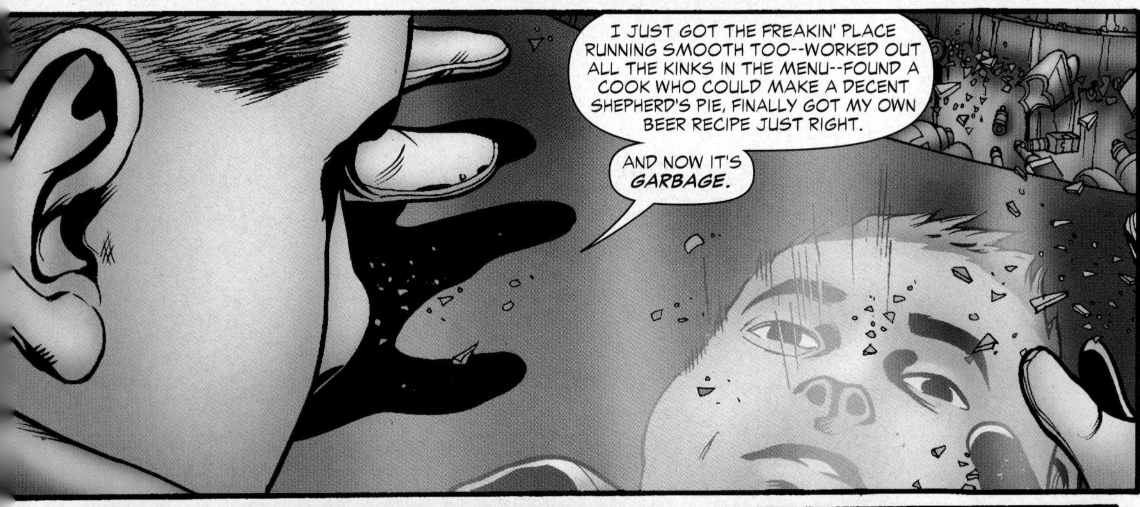
I JUST GOT THE FREAKIN' PLACE RUNNING SMOOTH TOO--WORKED OUT ALL THE KINKS IN THE MENU--FOUND A COOK WHO COULD MAKE A DECENT SHEPHERD'S PIE, FINALLY GOT MY OWN BEER RECIPE JUST RIGHT.
AND NOW IT'S GARBAGE.

I DON'T SEE GARBAGE.
YEAH, WHADDYA SEE?
I SEE A PLACE THAT JUST NEEDS TO BE CLEANED UP AND FIXED.

HELL, THERE'S A LOTTA SPOTS ON OA RIGHT NOW THAT ARE WAY HIGHER ON THE PRIORITY LIST THAN THIS ELBOW-BENDER.
NO, THERE'S NOT.
I THINK IT NEEDS TO BE AT THE TOP OF THE LIST.
YOU DO, HUH? AND WHY'S THAT?
BECAUSE WE ALL NEED A PLACE TO COME TO MORE THAN EVER SO WE CAN CONNECT TO EACH OTHER WITHOUT HAVING TO BE IN THE MIDDLE OF A FIREFIGHT--
--A PLACE WHERE WE CAN FORGET ABOUT ALL THE BAD STUFF WE'RE SEEING IN EACH AND EVERY CORNER OF THE UNIVERSE EVEN IF IT'S ONLY FOR A LITTLE WHILE.
THIS PLACE IS A GOOD THING, GUY. IT'S A VALUABLE THING. AND YOU BETTER REBUILD IT.
YOU CAN COUNT ON IT, CHUCKLES.
I KNOW WE CAN.
SHLAG
ATTENTION ALL LANTERNS. THE THIRD LAW STATING THAT PHYSICAL RELATIONSHIPS AND LOVE BETWEEN MEMBERS OF THE GREEN LANTERN CORPS IS FORBIDDEN HAS, FROM THIS MOMENT FORTH, BEEN REPEALED.
ATTENTION ALL LANTERNS. THE THIRD LAW STATING THAT PHYSICAL RELATIONSHIPS AND LOVE BETWEEN MEMBERS OF THE GREEN LANTERN CORPS IS FORBIDDEN HAS, FROM THIS MOMENT FORTH, BEEN REPEALED.
ATTENTION ALL LANTERNS. THE THIRD LAW STATING THAT PHYSICAL RELATIONSHIPS AND LOVE BETWEEN MEMBERS OF THE GREEN LANTERN CORPS IS FORBIDDEN HAS, FROM THIS MOMENT FORTH, BEEN REPEALED.
HRRM.

WHADDYA KNOW, THE BLUE MEANIES STILL GOT SOME HEART LEFT IN 'EM AFTER ALL.
AND SPEAKING OF HEARTS, I'M SURE THERE'S A DOCTOR "FRIEND" OF MINE SMILING RIGHT ABOUT NOW.
WELL, HERE'S TO THE BIG W, A PLACE WHERE EVERYBODY KNOWS YOUR NAME.
THE BIG W.
KLINK
AND HERE'S TO US, AND THOSE LIKE US.
KLINK
DAMN FEW, BUDDY. DAMN FEW.
END

BLACKEST NIGHT
GREEN LANTERN CORPS
VARIANT COVER GALLERY

GREEN LANTERN CORPS 39
Cover by Joe Jusko
JUSKO 09

GREEN LANTERN CORPS 40
Cover by Billy Tucci and Randy Mayor

GREEN LANTERN CORPS 41

Cover by Greg Horn

GREEN LANTERN CORPS 42
Cover by Greg Horn

GREEN LANTERN CORPS 43
Cover by Ladrönn

GREEN LANTERN CORPS 44
Cover by Greg Horn

GREEN LANTERN CORPS 45
Cover by Brian Bolland

GREEN LANTERN CORPS 46
Cover by Greg Horn

RMIGLIARI X

CKEST NIGHT —

d Black Lantern Kilowog Cover

When Nekron turned the heroes who had escaped death before into Black Lanterns we almost turned Kilowog as well, but instead decided to focus on Earth heroes.

Painted art by Greg Horn.

BLACK LANTERN ICE

ALTER EGO: TORA OLAFSDOTTER
TORA'S POWERS ARE SUGGESTED BY HER NAME. BUT HER FREEZING ABILITIES COULD NOT HELP HER WHEN SHE WAS MURDERED BY THE OVERMASTER. ICE WAS MYSTERIOUSLY RESURRECTED, ALLOWING NEKRON TO GAIN A HOLD ON HER, TRANSFORMING HER INTO A BLACK LANTERN WHOSE MAIN GOAL IS THE DESTRUCTION OF HER BELOVED GUY GARDNER.

Design by Joe Prado

BLACK LANTERN JADE

ALTER EGO: JENNIFER-LYNN HAYDEN
JADE, A FORMER GREEN LANTERN AND THE DAUGHTER OF ALAN SCOTT, MET HER END AT THE HANDS OF ALEXANDER LUTHOR, JR. RETURNING AS A BLACK LANTERN, JADE HAS SET OFF AFTER HER FORMER BOYFRIEND, KYLE RAYNER.

Design by Joe Prado

BLACK LANTERN KILOWOG UNUSED

ALTER EGO: GREEN LANTERN
THE DRILL SERGEANT OF THE GREEN LANTERN CORPS WAS SLAIN BY THE PARALLAX-POSSESSED HAL JORDAN BUT WAS LATER RETURNED TO THE LAND OF THE LIVING BY KYLE RAYNER AND GANTHET. NEKRON WAS UNABLE TO TURN KILOWOG AS HE WAS NOT ON EARTH AT THE TIME OF NEKRON'S STRIKE.

Design by Joe Prado

RED LANTERN GUY GARDNER

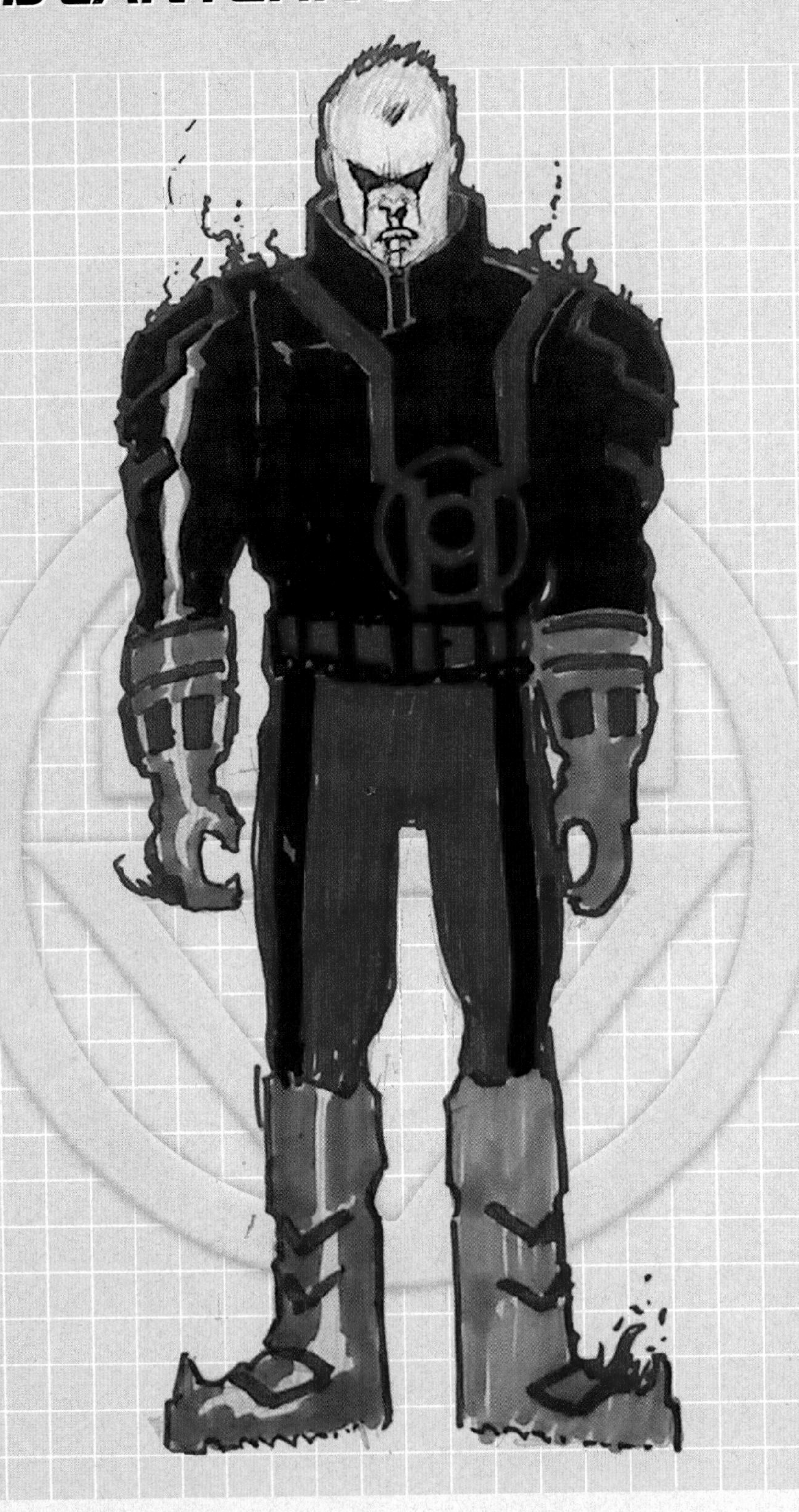

ALTER EGO: GREEN LANTERN
GUY GARDNER BELIEVES HIMSELF TO BE THE GREATEST GREEN LANTERN OF THEM ALL. HIS WILLPOWER LITERALLY SPARKS FROM THE RING, BUT HIS EGOTISTICAL PERSONALITY COULD PREVENT HIM FROM EVER REACHING THE HEIGHTS OF FELLOW EARTH LANTERN HAL JORDAN. HIS INTENSE ANGER GOT THE BETTER OF HIM WHEN HE BELIEVED THAT HIS COMRADE KYLE RAYNER WAS DEAD, ALLOWING HIM TO BE OVERTAKEN BY A CRIMSON RING OF RAGE.

Design by Patrick Gleason

BIOGRAPHIES

PETER J. TOMASI

Peter J. Tomasi was an editor with DC Comics for many years where he proudly helped usher in new eras for GREEN LANTERN, BATMAN, and JSA. He is now solely devoting all his time to writing comics and screenplays, having worked on such DC titles as GREEN LANTERN CORPS, BATMAN: BLACKEST NIGHT, THE OUTSIDERS, NIGHTWING, BLACK ADAM, and the critically acclaimed graphic novel LIGHT BRIGADE along with many other stories. His current projects include GREEN LANTERN: EMERALD WARRIORS and co-writing the bi-weekly series BRIGHTEST DAY.

PATRICK GLEASON

Patrick Gleason's career in comics has included work for Marvel and Image Comics. He is most noted for illustrating DC Comics' AQUAMAN, the relaunch of the Green Lantern Corps mini series, RECHARGE, and the regular ongoing GREEN LANTERN CORPS series. He is currently working on the follow-up to BLACKEST NIGHT, BRIGHTEST DAY.

REBECCA BUCHMAN

Rebecca Buchman has been involved with the comics industry since 2007 and lives in the Atlanta, Georgia metropolitan area. She learned her craft by studying under inker Dexter Vines. When she's not working on comics, Rebecca can be found kayaking, skiing and motorcycling.

FOLLOW THE COMPLETE

SAGA IN THESE GRAPHIC NOVELS

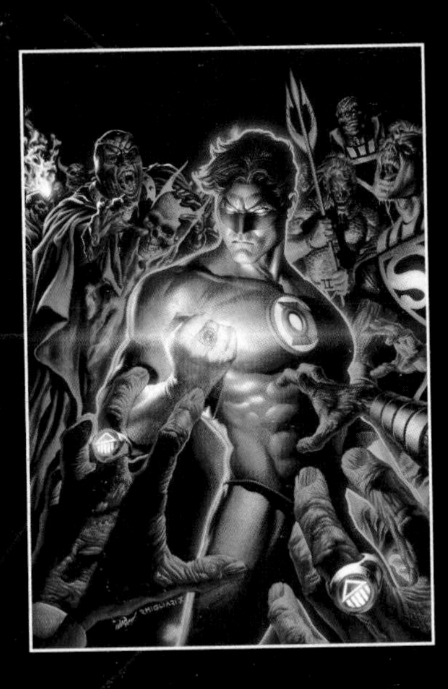

BLACKEST NIGHT
Geoff Johns & Ivan Reis

BLACKEST NIGHT: GREEN LANTERN
Geoff Johns & Doug Mahnke

BLACKEST NIGHT: GREEN LANTERN CORPS
Peter J. Tomasi & Patrick Gleason

BLACKEST NIGHT: BLACK LANTERN CORPS VOL. 1
Peter J. Tomasi, James Robinson, J.T. Krul, Ardian Syaf, Ed Benes & Eddy Barrows

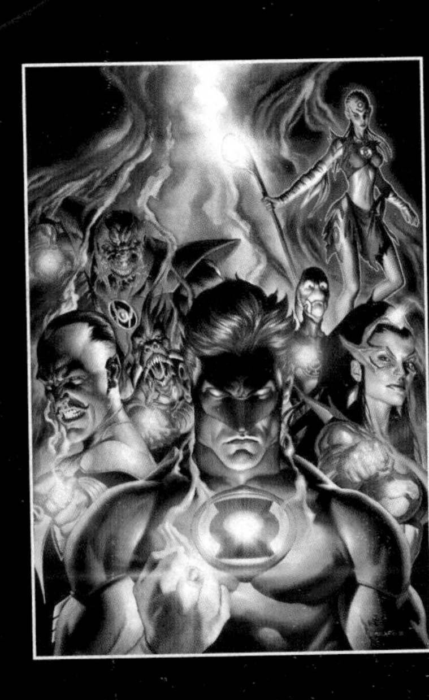

BLACKEST NIGHT: BLACK LANTERN CORPS VOL. 2
Geoff Johns, James Robinson, Greg Rucka, Scott Kolins, Eddy Barrows & Nicola Scott

BLACKEST NIGHT: RISE OF THE BLACK LANTERNS
Geoff Johns, Peter J. Tomasi, James Robinson & others

BLACKEST NIGHT: TALES OF THE CORPS
Geoff Johns, Peter J. Tomasi & others